The FOOD of LOVE

The Taste of Shakespeare in Four Seasons

Alan Deegan and Alycia Smith-Howard

Graficas Books

First published 2012 by *Graficas Books,*
Cwmbach, Glasbury-on-Wye, Powys HR3 5LU

Main text set in Shakespeare Book and Poliphilus MT Std by *Graficas Design.*

Printed in Great Britain by *Gomer Press,* Llandysul Ceredigion SA44 4JL

ISBN 978-0-9554834-6-2

British Library Cataloguing in Publication Data.
A catalogue record for this book is available
from the British Library

The FOOD of LOVE

The Taste of Shakespeare in Four Seasons

The FOOD of LOVE

The Taste of Shakespeare in Four Seasons

Recipe Index

Except where stated the recipes are for 4 people.

Eating in Tudor England

Food played a large part in the life of of both gentry and peasants in the Elizabethan period. The gentry ate three good meals a day and the lower classes two but, while neither diets were particularly good nutritionally, on balance that of the poorer classes was more healthy and arguably better than that which many eat today. The rich ate vast amounts of meat with some vegetables, while the lower classes consumed lots of vegetables, fruits and potages ⁄ a type of soup. Vegetables were less popular with the rich who considered them to be suitable only for the lower classes.

In his book "*Compendyous Regyment or Dyetary of Health*", 1542, Andrew Boorde advised readers to eat vegetables and fruit but, as both were regarded with suspicion, they were mostly overcooked, thus losing valuable vitamins. The over cooking could be attributed to advice in the "*Boke of Kervynge*", 1500, which stated "*Beware of green sallettes and rawe fruytes for they wyll make your soverayne seke*". For this reason fruit sales were banned on the streets during the plague in 1569.

For all classes bread was the major part of the diet and everyone ate cheese, although dairy food was considered inferior and suitable only for the lower classes, but what was different was the quality of the product. Everyone drank ale, in preference to the polluted water, brewed without hops and not particularly alcoholic. Beer, which was brewed from hops, was cheaper than ale but not as popular. Wine, which was imported, was only drunk by the wealthy, cider being a drink of the poorer person. Perry and Mead was also drunk.

There was also no way to keep food fresh so meat had to be eaten in season or salted or pickled. The lower classes were not allowed to to hunt rabbit or deer, but were able to hunt wild pig, collect berries and take fish from rivers. While they were not allowed to cut wood, they were able to gather dead wood from trees and hedges if it could be collected with a hook or shepherd's crook, hence the expression "*By hook or by crook*".

By law fish had to be consumed three times a week. In addition to the religious requirement, it was done in order to keep the fishing fleet in repair as the sailors, making up part of the navy, were needed for service. In 1588 for instance, at the time of the Spanish Armada, only 92 ships could be mustered against 150 Spanish Galleons. It was only when private merchant ships were refitted that the fleet could be increased to 200 ships. The fish was not necessarily fresh as there were no quick way of transporting fresh food so, unless fished from the local river, it was most likely dried cod or salted herring.

Sugar was becoming increasingly popular with the gentry with the resultant increase in tooth decay. Blackened teeth, however, was considered a status symbol displaying the ability to afford sugary things, which were mostly cakes, marzipan or fruits in syrup. In some instance people blackened their teeth with ashes in order to be fashionable. To try to help prevent tooth decay, ashes from rosemary or powdered alabaster could be rubbed on the teeth with the finger. Silver tooth picks, which were kept in a hat, were used to clean teeth. In Shakespeare's The Winter's Tale, Clown was able to recognise "*A great man by the pickings on's teeth*".

Imported originally from Morocco and Barbary and then from Portugal and Spain, from their plantations in the West Indies, sugar was refined in London, where there had been a refinery from the 1540s, making the raw product into cones weighing 14 pounds. The national average of yearly sugar consumption per head during the Elizabethan period was only one pound and was mostly eaten by the gentry.

Tableware during the period consisted of a knife and spoon. Food was cut with a knife and eaten with fingers. Stews, soups and bruets could be eaten with a spoon.

Breakfast
Many wealthy people ate '*manchets*', a type of large loaf, which was a creamy colour and made from wheat flour with a little added wheatgerm and bran. It was round, weighed about six pounds and spread with butter to make it more palatable. Eggs were also eaten and simply cooked being beaten and cooked like scambled egg or an omelette. Beef was also sometimes eaten by the better-off.

The lower classes ate bread and eggs or porridge and meat, if it could be obtained. The dark brown or black '*Carter's Bread*' was the bread of the lower classes and was made of rye and wheat, called '*maslin*', or from '*drage*', a mixture of wheat and barley, or from rye alone.

The middle classes ate '*Ravel*' or '*Yeoman's Bread*', less expensive and darker than manchet and made from a coarser whole-wheat flour in which the the bran was left.

Dinner
The mid-day meal was eaten from ten o'clock and could take up to three hours for the gentry. The lower classes would eat from ten in the morning until noon and again in the late evening.

Supper
This meal was much the same as dinner for the gentry, with dishes of game – feathered and venison, fish, oysters and lobster, beef, veal, capon, rabbit, possibly salad and vegetables, fruit tarts and cheese.

For the merchant or middle classes dinner could include sausage, pike, stewed carp, woodcock, roasted blackbird, cabbage and porridge. The lower classes had much coarser foods, stews, types of sausage and raw, or overcooked, vegetables, pottage, some fish and, if possible, some meat.

The Tudor period was a time of change in virtually every aspect of life and culture and food was no exception. The Renaissance was in full swing in Europe and new foods, such as tomatoes, potatoes and turkey, were being brought back to England from the New World by Privateers and Merchant Ships.

> **"Cheer and great welcome makes a merry feast!"**
>
> *Comedy of Errors*

Samuel Johnson called Shakespeare's works "a Map of Life." Without a doubt, food is an essential part of the journey. And, being the great master-revealer of life in all its myriad shapes and forms, Shakespeare's works unsurprisingly provide a window into the culinary delights of the world that surrounded him.

There are no less than 2,000 culinary references in Shakespeare's plays and poems. His last, and some would argue his greatest, work *The Tempest*, is one of my all-time top Shakespeare favourites, not least because of the celebration and sumptious banquet that magically materialise toward the end of the play.

First, Prospero's daughter, Miranda, and her new-found love Ferdinand are blessed and honoured by the great goddess Ceres ("*Most bounteous lady of wheat, rye, barley, oats and peas!*"), shortly after this, Prospero's enemies are tempted with a lavish feast beyond their wildest dreams, which vanishes just as the rare delicacies are about to touch their famished lips! Marvelous stuff.

This is just one example of the dozens of instances of dining and feasting that occurs in Shakespeare's incredible works. The word 'feast' itself, in fact, appears over 100 times throughout the plays. And, for me, Shakespeare has always been a feast for the senses.

I discovered Shakespeare as a child. When, at the age 6, I rather naughtily pinched a record from my parents' treasured record collection. It was an album of a well-known actor reading excerpts from Shakespeare's *A Midsummer Night's Dream*. My act of mischief was met with evocative sounds of that delightful mischief-maker, Puck. I was enchanted, completely hooked from that tender moment on. And, I've never looked back.

My journey with Shakespeare since that time has been quite a remarkable one, and one full of surprises, the joy of discovery and the unexpected. One such unexpected joy has been that of the opportunity to collaborate with Chef Alan Deegan. A scholar, a showman, a teacher and a believer, Alan has the culinary magic of Prospero, the mercurial energy (and mischief!) of Puck, and the down-to-earth good humour and wisdom of Bottom the Weaver – all rolled into one!

Alan encouraged me, to paraphrase a quote from the Chorus of *Henry V*, to 'work, work my thoughts', and take on the challenge of seeing Shakespeare from a fresh and foodie perspective, in addition to my customary literary and theatrical one. And, what a delicious treat it has been!

Alycia Smith-Howard

Foreword

I have known Alan for over twenty years and what I have noticed over that time is his dedication to educating people about to enter the hospitality industry.

Alan has set himself the task of making sure that the culinary skills of past generations are not lost to today's cooks. The traditions and craft are high on his agenda for his students. He sources excellent work placements where these skills can be honed by his students.

I am not at all surprised by this book, combining the works of William Shakespeare and 16th Century recipes being updated for the twenty first century, because it is just integrating Alan's two main interests, history and the culinary arts ∕ after all he was Head of Catering at Stratford Upon Avon College.

The recipes in *"The Food of Love"* are a collection of 16th Century recipes which have been developed into lighter dishes which suits today's palate, he has rediscovered recipes using flowers, in salads and main dishes and sweets, not just for garnish and eye appeal but for the delicate flavours they bring to the dishes.

The Food of Love is a comprehensive compendium of dishes, including, soups, fish, meat, poultry and game, salads, sweets, bread, cheese and drinks. All of which started their culinary life in Elizabethan England.
The book encompasses the essence of what Alan instills in his students, flavours, culinary techniques, seasonal food and variety.

All of the recipes have been designed so as to be easily accomplished and will make entertaining at home a joy.

Martyn Nail
Executive Chef Claridge's
November 2012

Bibliography

The Boke of Keruynge	Wynkyn de Worde
English Bread and Yeast Cookery	Elizabeth David
Food in England	Dorothy Hartley
Food and Cooking in 16th Century Britain	Peter Brears
Food and Cooking in Medieval Britain	Maggie Black
The Art of Cooking Made Plain and Easy	Hannah Glasse
A Compendyous Regyment or Dyetary of Helth	Andrew Boorde
Food and Drink in Tudor England	Tim Lambert
The Boke of Nurture	John Russell
Food in History	Reay Tannahill

Acknowledgements

Forbes McQueen ⁄ *A M Bailley Fruits & Vegetables.*

Alan Healey ⁄ *Aubrey Allen Butchers.*

Jeremy Collar ⁄ *M&J Seafoods.*

Jeremy Bowen and David Jowett ⁄ *Paxton & Whitfield Artisan Cheese.*

Stratford Upon Avon College ⁄ especially Elizabeth Lefeuvre, Stores Manager.

Sam Bostock and Chris Carson ⁄ Advanced Culinary Diploma Students.

My dear wife Daveda ⁄ a true inspiration.

Alycia for the spark of this idea.

Tom and Jane Allwright ⁄ *Graficas Design,* for all the advice and help,
and Tom for the photography.

SPRING

"**Speak of the spring and the rich harvest of the year.**" — Sonnet #53

For Shakespeare, Spring was a jovial time of love and romance, as he wrote in the following song, "Spring," from the play, *Love's Labours Lost*:

> It was a lover and his lass,
> With hey, and a ho, and a hey nonino,
> That o'er the green corn field did pass,
> In the Spring time, the only pretty ring time,
> When birds do sing, hey ding a ding,
> Sweet lovers love the Spring.
>
> Between the acres of the rye,
> With hey, and a ho, and a hey nonino,
> These pretty country folks would lie,
> In the Spring time, the only pretty ring time,
> When birds do sing, hey ding a ding, ding,
> Sweet lovers love the Spring.
>
> This carol they began that hour,
> With hey, and a ho, and a hey nonino,
> How that life was but a flower,
> In the Spring time, the only pretty ring time,
> When birds do sing, hey ding a ding, ding,
> Sweet lovers love the Spring.
>
> And therefore take the present time,
> With hey, and a ho, and a hey nonino,
> For love is crowned with the prime,
> In the Spring time, the only pretty ring time,
> When birds do sing, hey ding a ding, ding,
> Sweet lovers love the Spring.

Shakespeare captures the spirit of the gleeful season in his comedy, *As You Like It,* which is one of Shakespeare's most popular plays. The play's heroine, Rosalind, is arguably his most dazzling female character.

Rosalind is the daughter of a banished duke who falls in love with Orlando, the disinherited son of one of the duke's friends. When she is banished from the court by her usurping uncle, Duke Frederick, Rosalind takes on the appearance of a boy, calling herself Ganymede. She travels with her cousin Celia, and the jester Touchstone into the Forest of Arden, where her father and his friends live in exile.

In this pastoral world of shepherds and shepherdesses, love blossoms, new friends are made, and families are reunited. Some of Shakespeare's most poetic language flows throughout the play as a series of merry and melancholy misunderstandings and mistaken identities unfold in the forest. In the end, the force of true love conquers all, and there is a quadruple wedding of Rosalind and Orlando, Oliver and Celia, Silvius and Phebe, and Touchstone and Audrey.

A time of new beginnings and fledging love, Spring was also a time of celebration and feasting, with pancakes and fritters taking the fore in Shrove Tuesday.

> **"As fit as a pancake for Shrove Tuesday!"**
>
> *– All's Well That Ends Well*

William Fennor, a contemporary of Shakespeare's, observed the merry-making on this festive day:

> **Every stomache till it can hold no more,**
> **Is fritter-filled, as well as heart can wish;**
> **And every man and maide doe take their turne,**
> **And tosse their pancakes up for feare they burne;**
> **And all the kitchen doth with laughter sound,**
> **To see the pancakes fall upon the ground.**

The recipes in the chapter will enable you to recreate the gaiety of Spring anytime of year.

Celebrations in Spring

Spring is the time when the earth is revived, budding trees, shoots appear and new growth is everywhere. Spring showers (bring May flowers) and the sun, help to regenerate the countryside. There is much work to be done on the land with the sowing of fresh seed and tilling the soil.

Spring vegetables and fruits are a delight and the brighter days make us all feel alive again after the gloom of winter. Spring lamb, chicken and young vegetables, which are all in abundance, appear on menus everywhere. Flowers are readily available and can be used in many ways.

Festivals of Spring include :

Ash Wednesday, traditionally a day of repentance and the first day of Lent, the forehead was smeared with ashes to denote repentance.

St George's Day, April 23rd, is also Shakespeare's birthday and the anniversary of his death. St. George's day in England is celebrated by the wearing of a red rose and telling tales of St. George fighting the dragon. It is said that he was a Roman soldier who stood up for the Christians who were being tortured and killed - in doing so, and for his deeds in helping Christians, he was put to death.

Mothering Sunday, the fourth Sunday in Lent. Traditionally it was a day when female domestic servants were given a day off to visit their mothers and family. Centuries ago it was considered very important for people to return to their "mother" church once a year, which also meant that people would meet up with their families. Children would also give their mothers flowers to celebrate the reunion.

Good Friday, also called "Holy Friday or Black Friday or Great Friday", is the day on which Christians commemorate the death of Jesus. Traditionally in England hot cross buns are eaten.

Easter Sunday, also called Easter Day and Resurrection Day, on which Christians celebrate the resurrection of Jesus. Chocolate eggs are supposed to represent the stone being rolled away from the entrance to his tomb.

May Day, also called the Feast of Beltane and the Festival of Flora, (or Floralia). All of the festivals celebrate the rebirth of the land.

All of the dishes chosen for this section have been selected to reflect the warm spring sun with seasonal ingredients all based on original 16th century recipes. The section on salads and flowers are particularly spring like.

TheFOOD of LOVE

The Taste of Shakespeare in Four Seasons

Spring Season Index

To Make a Hodgepodge

Boyle a neck of mutton or a fat rump of beef , and when it be boyled take the best of the broth and put it into a pipkin and put a good many onions to it, two handfull of marigold flowers, and a handfull of percely fine picked and groce shredde and not too small and so boyle them in the broth and thicke it with strained bread, putting therin groce beaten pepper, and a spoonful of vinagre, let it boyle somewhat thicke and so lay it upon your meat.

Spring Hodgepodge

Ingredients

200g	Neck of Lamb - diced small	25g	Carrot - cut into fine strips
25g	Leek - cut into fine strips	25g	Celery - peeled and cut into fine strips
50g	Onion - sliced	25g	Turnip - cut in fine strips
50g	Potato - cut into small dice	5g	Parsley - chopped
1ltr	White Lamb or Chicken Stock	2	Marigold Petals - shredded

Method

1. Place the lamb in cold water, bring to boil and refresh under running cold water.
2. Put lamb and vegetables, except the potatoes, into a pan with the stock.
3. Bring to the boil and skim off any scum, check seasoning and cook for ½ hour. Add the potatoes and cook for a further 15 minutes, check seasoning and add the parsley.
4. Garnish with some of the shredded marigold petals.

3

Parsnip and Apple Soup with Smoked Oysters

Ingredients

1ltr	Chicken Stock	**30g**	Salt Free Butter
300g	Parsnips - peeled and chopped	**150g**	Potato - peeled and chopped
60g	Onion - chopped	**150g**	Apples - peeled, cored and diced
Pinch	Saffron	**Sprig**	Dill
4	Smoked Oysters - well drained and dried on kitchen paper		

Method

1. Sweat the onion in the butter, then add the parsnip and cook for 2 minutes.
2. Add the stock and bring to the boil, add the potatoes and apple, re-boil and add the saffron and season.
3. Cook for 30 minutes until the potatoes and the parsnips are soft.
4. Blend the soup in a liquidizer and return to the pan. Re-boil, add the cream and check the seasoning and consistency of the soup. Place the oysters in the soup and reheat them for 10 minutes.
5. Serve one oyster with each portion, garnished with the dill.

Salmon Salad with Pippins

Ingredients

300g	Poached Salmon - marinaded in lemon juice and olive oil		
60g	Onion - very finely diced	60g	Grated Apple
10g	Dill - chopped fine	10g	Capers
60g	Mayonnaise	Pinch	Ground Ginger
150g	Mixed Salad Leaves	100ml	Olive Oil
60g	Tomato - skinned and chopped pips removed		

Tomato dressing, Seasoning – salt, pepper, sugar, vinegar

Method

1. Drain and flake the salmon into a bowl, wrap the onion in a cloth and wash under running hot water, squeeze dry. Add to the salmon.
2. Add the apple and season with pepper and ginger.
3. Mix in the mayonnaise and refrigerate until required.
4. Blend the olive oil and tomato in a liquidizer and season with salt, pepper, sugar and vinegar.
5. To serve, place some of the salmon mixture in an oiled 3 inch cutter ring or mould and tamp down, sprinkle the top with dill. Repeat four times.
6. Place the salmon on a plate and remove the mould, garnish with the salad leaves, sprinkle capers around the plate and drizzle some of the tomato dressing around the salmon.

To Crimp a Cod

Take a gallon of pump water and a pound of salt, mix them well together; take your cod whilst alive and cut it in slices of one and a half inches thick, throw it into the salt and water for half an hour; then take it out and dry it well with a clean cloth, flour it and broil it; or have a stew pan with some pump water and salt boiling, put in your fish and boil it quickly for five minutes; send oyster sauce, anchovy sauce, shrimp sauce or what sauce you please. Garnish with horse radish and green parsley.

Cod with Mushrooms and Horseradish

Ingredients

400g	Cod Fillet - skinned, pin boned and cut into 4 portions		
100g	Oyster Mushrooms - sliced	60g	Finely Diced Shallot
100ml	Dry White Wine	200ml	Fish Stock
30g	Salt Free Butter	10 fl oz	Double Cream
1 tspn	Creamed Horseradish	Sprig	Chervil

Method

1. In a shallow pan sweat the shallot in the butter, add the mushrooms and cook for 2 – 3 minutes.
2. Place the washed cod on top of the mushrooms and add the fish stock and wine.
3. Cover with a lid and cook for 8 – 10 minutes.
4. When cooked, remove the cod and keep it warm and well drained.
5. Reduce the cooking liquor by 2/3 and add the cream and horse radish. Reduce by ½ and check seasoning.
6. Place some of the mushrooms on the plate and place the cod on top, drizzle the sauce over the fish and garnish with the chervil.

6

Spiced Herring in a Orange Marinade

Ingredients

4	Small Herring - filleted and pin boned		30g	Shallot - chopped
200ml	Orange Juice		Pinch	Ground Mace
Pinch	Ground Nutmeg		Pinch	Ground Ginger
5g	Fresh Ginger - cut in fine strips		30g	Salt Free Butter
4	Pansy Heads			

Method

1. Sweat the shallot and the ginger in the butter. Add the orange juice.
2. Dust the herring with the spices and season with salt and pepper.
3. Place the herring in with the orange juice and cover with a lid bring to boil and remove from heat.
4. When cold refrigerate for as long as possible.
5. To serve place the herring fillet on the plate and strain some of the marinade over the fish.
6. Serve with some salad leaves & garnish with the pansy heads.

Crimped Turbot in a Sorrel Sauce

Ingredients

4	150g Slices of Turbot fillet		30g	Shallots - fine diced
100g	Sorrel - finely shredded		100ml	Dry White Wine
30g	Salt Free Butter		200ml	Double Cream
1	Lemon Zest - in fine strips		Sprig	Chervil

Method

1. Sweat the shallot in the butter, add the wine, sorrel and cream. Season and reduce by half.
2. Mark the turbot in a griddle pan to make a nice trellis pattern, cook on each side for 4 minutes.
3. Place turbot on a tray and keep warm.
4. Check the sauce for seasoning and finish with a little butter.
5. Pour sauce onto a plate and place turbot on top of the sauce.
6. Garnish with the chervil and lemon zest.

Observations on Pies

Raised pies should have a quick oven and well closed up, or your pie will fall in the sides; it should have no water put in till it goes in to the oven, it makes the crust sad, and is a great hazard of the pie running.

To Make A Savoury Meat Pie

Make a good puff paste crust, cut your meet into pieces, season it to your palate with pepper, salt, mace, nutmeg, cloves, finely beat; lay it into your crust with oysters and forcemeat balls, set all over with butter and lay on your crust and set it in a quick oven an hour and a half, have ready your liquor made thus, 1 pint of gravy, the oyster liquor and a gill of red wine, mix all together with the yolks of two or three eggs, beat and keep it stirring one way, when it boils pour it into your pie, send it hot to table.

Beef Steak Pie with Mushrooms

Ingredients

500g	Diced Chuck Steak	120g	Chopped Onion
200g	Button Mushrooms - cut in ¼	1tspn	Anchovy Fillets - chopped fine
½ tspn	Worcester Sauce	4 fl oz	Good Beef Stock
4 fl oz	Madeira Wine	1 tspn	Tarragon - chopped
200g	Puff Pastry	1	Egg

Seasoning - Salt, Pepper, Mace, Nutmeg, to taste

Method

1. Mix the meat, onion, mushrooms, anchovy, Worcester sauce, seasoning and wine stock together.
2. Place in a pie dish and cover with the puff pastry. Beat the egg, add a pinch of salt and egg wash the pastry. Rest the pastry for 1 hour.
3. Bake in a hot oven, after 15 minutes the pastry should be set and the oven can be turned down to a moderate temperature - 150c for 2 hours.

Pork Olives with Raisins in a Cider Sauce

Ingredients

500g	Pork Fillet	120g	Raisins
120g	Breadcrumbs	1	Egg
Pinch	Ground Ginger	Pinch	Cinnamon
60g	Grated Apple	30g	Salt Free Butter
250ml	Cider	250ml	Good Brown Beef or Chicken Stock
1tspn	Cornflour	30g	Shallot - chopped

Seasoning

Method

1. Cut the pork into 4 pieces.
2. Place each piece between some plastic sheet (cling film or a plastic bag) and beat the pork flat with a meat hammer.
3. Take the breadcrumbs, raisins and grated apple and mix together, bind with the egg, season with the spices.
4. Place the raisin and apple mix into the centre and roll up to form a big sausage. Roll the pork in cling film and tie each end tightly. Poach in boiling water for about 10 minutes and then rest the pork in the cling film for 10 minutes, keeping it warm.
5. Sweat the shallot in a little butter, add the stock and cider, boil and reduce by half.
6. Remove the pork from the cling film, drain and keep warm.
7. Slacken the cornflour with a little water and whisk into the boiling sttock. Re-boil and it will thicken, check the seasoning and pass through a fine strainer.
8. Cut the pork olive in four, arrange two on each plate and pour over the sauce.

Fricassee of Turkey with Peppers and Chillies

Ingredients

400g	Diced Turkey Meat	**100g**	Chopped Onion
2	Red Peppers - de-seeded and diced small		
2	Red Chillies - de-seeded and chopped small		
2	Cloves Garlic - crushed to a paste		
60g	Salt Free Butter	**100ml**	Chicken Stock
100ml	Dry Sherry	**325ml**	Double Cream
1 tspn	Chopped Tarragon	**8**	Chives - whole

Method

1. Sweat the onion, peppers and chillies in the butter until soft.
2. Add the turkey meat and seal, add the sherry and reduce by half.
3. Add the cream and stock, boil and check seasoning, cover with a lid.
4. Cook for 1 hour and check if cooked.
5. Check seasoning and consistency. Sprinkle the tarragon on top. Garnish with some chives.
6. Serve with some rice or cous cous and salad.

To Make Syllabub From The Cow

Make your syllabub from either cider or wine, sweeten it pretty sweet and grate nutmeg in; then milk the milk into Liquor; when this is done, pour over the top half a pint or pint of cream according to the amount of syllabub you make. You may make this syllabub at home, only have new milk, make it as hot as milk from the cow, and out of a pot pour it in holding your hand very high and strew over some currants well washed and picked plumped up before the fire.

Lime and Champagne Syllabub

Ingredients

200ml	Double Cream
75g	Caster Sugar
2	Limes' Juice and Zest – cut into thin strips
100ml	Champagne
4	Crystalized Violets
4 small	Mint Leaves

Method

1. Whisk the cream, sugar and lime juice in a bowl.
2. Gradually incorporate the Champagne.
3. Whisk to a peak, pipe into glasses and chill until required.
4. Cook the strips of zest in a little water with a teaspoon of sugar until soft and sticky, cool.
5. Decorate the syllabub with the violets, the mint leaves and the zest.

Pear Pancakes with Ginger Confit

Ingredients

Pancake Batter

2	Eggs	10fl oz	Milk
Pinch	Ground Ginger	**Pinch**	Salt
100g	Flour	**15g**	Melted Butter

Whisk all together, strain and put to rest in the fridge. Add the melted butter.

Filling

120g	Pear - peeled cored and diced	30g	Sugar
30g	Butter	**2 tspn**	Apricot Jam

Sweat the pear in the butter, add the sugar and cook till the pear is soft. Add the apricot jam.

Confit

60g	Stem Ginger - chopped	100ml	Ginger Wine
30g	Sugar	**50ml**	Orange Juice

Boil all together until thick and sticky.

Method

1. In a non-stick pan heat a little oil - only enough to coat the bottom of the pan thinly.
2. Pour in enough batter to cover the bottom of the pan, cook until bubbles appear. Turn the pancake over and cook for 1 minute.
3. Repeat the above until you have 8 pancakes.
4. Lay the warm pancake on a plate, fill with the pear mixture and roll up or fold.
5. Place some of the confit by the side of the pancakes and dust with icing sugar.

Caramelized Apples with Blancmange

Ingredients

Blancmange

450ml	Whipping Cream	50g	Cornflour
50g	Caster Sugar	½ tspn	Vanilla Extract or Vanilla Seeds

Method

1. Dilute the cornflour with a little water.
2. Boil the cream, sugar and vanilla.
3. Whisk the diluted cornflour into the cream, re-boil for 2 – 3 minutes.
4. Pour into a greased Dariol mould and chill.

Caramelized Apples

2	Dessert Apples peeled, cored and cut into ½ cm wedges		
60g	Caster Sugar	60g	Salt free Butter
1 tblsp	Lemon Juice	2 tblsp	Brandy
4	Pansy Heads		

Method

1. Melt the butter in a frying pan, add the sugar and caramelize.
2. Add the apples and cook until coated, remove from heat, add the brandy and lemon juice and cool.

Assembling the dish

1. Very gently ease the cornflour mixture away from the sides of the mould with your fingers.
2. Turn out onto a plate, arrange apples to one side and pour some of the syrup over the mould.
3. Garnish with a mint leaf.

Vegetables Available in Spring

Carrots, Broccoli, Endive, Cabbages, Lettuce, Beetroot, Garlic, Parsnips, Celery, Potatoes, Sorrel, Oyster Plant, Onions, Young Onions, Shallots, Radish, Spinach.

Recipes and suggestions may be found in the Vegetable and Salad section.

Kissing Comfits,
or
Perfumed Lozenges

Instructions

Take twelve grains of Ambergreece, and six grains of Musk, and beat it with some Sugar plate spoken of before, then roule it out in thin Cakes, and make them into what form you please, you may make them round like a Sugar Plumb, and put a Coriander seed in each of them, and so they will be fine Comfits, and you may make them into Lozenges with which to perfume Wine.

Sweet Perfumed Kisses

Ingredients

275g	Icing Sugar	3	Tblsp. Double Cream
3	Tblsp. Violet Syrup	20	Crystalized Violets

Method

1. Mix the icing sugar, cream and syrup together to a smooth paste.
2. Roll out on a dusting of icing sugar and cut into required shape.
3. If desired coat in chocolate and decorate with the violets.

SUMMER

"Think on fantastic summer's heat"

– Richard II

Of all the seasons, Summer seems to have been Shakespeare's clear favourite. Some of his most beautiful poetry commemorates this glorious, sultry season:

Shall I compare thee to a summer's day? Thou art more lovely and temperate:
Rough winds do shake the darling buds of May, and summer's lease hath all too short a date.

– Sonnet #18

Shakespeare's high-spirited comedy, *A Midsummer Night's Dream* is a tribute to the blithe and sensuous essence of this season. At the centre of the play are four, young, Athenian lovers (Helena, Hermia, Lysander and Demetrius), and a group of tradesmen who are also amateur actors, (including Bottom, the Weaver). The action of the play details the lovers' and the tradesmen's interactions with the Duke of Athens, Theseus, the Queen of the Amazons, Hippolyta, and with the fairies who inhabit an enchanted, moonlit forest.

The fairy world, ruled by Oberon and Titania, is out of sorts, and the human beings who stumble into this realm become entangled, unwittingly in the regal quarrel of the Fairy King and Queen. Oberon's mischievous sprite, Puck, creates merry chaos in this tale of friendship, love, and mistaken identity. Full of outrageous high jinks, *A Midsummer Night's Dream* is one of Shakespeare's most popular works, and is a perennial favourite on stage and screen.

Shakespeare drew inspiration for this work from the traditions and celebrations of the Summer Solstice and Midsummer Eve. In Shakespeare's day, Midsummer Eve (June 23) was celebrated as a jocular and lively occasion with blazing bonfires, revelry and feasting. Midsummer was a magical time. It was believed that fairies danced at midnight on Midsummer Eve and so many caroused into the wee hours of the night in an attempt to see them. Writing in the late fifteenth century, John Mirk, the Prior of Lilleshall Abbey, in Shropshire, warned his fellow priests to stand against this time of –

"songs, dances, and gluttony."

Like Shakespeare's vivacious play and the irrepressible Midsummer celebrations, the recipes in this section encapsulate the gaiety and vitality of this ebullient season.

The time will bring on summer,
When briers shall have leaves as well as thorns,
And be as sweet as sharp.

– All's Well that Ends Well

The FOOD of LOVE

The Taste of Shakespeare
in Four Seasons

Summer Season Index

Chilled Green Pea Soup
Chilled Cherry and Rose Soup
Tian of Smoked Eel and Asparagus
Fricassee of Sole with Mushrooms and Saffron Cream
Buttered Crab with Whisky and Ginger
Gratin of Plaice with Garlic and Shallot Marmalade
Poached Breast of Duck with Quince and Lemon Confit
Chicken Pie
Fillet of Lamb with Rosemary and Creamed Leeks
Lemon Possett and Summer Berries
Strawberry and Lavender Jelly
Almond Ice Cream with Compote of Cherries

A Green Peas Soup

Take a knuckle of veal and one pound of lean ham, cut them in thin slices, lay the ham at the bottom of a soup pot, the veal upon the ham; then cut six onions in slices and put on, two or three turnips, two carrots, tree heads of celery cut small, a little thyme, four cloves and four blades of mace; put a little water at the bottom, cover the pot close, and draw it gently but do not let it stick; then put in six quarts of boiling water, let it stew gently for four hours, and skim it well; take two quarts of green peas and stew them in some of the broth till tender; then strain them off, and put them in a marble mortar, and beat them fine, put the liquor in and mix them up (if you have no mortar, you must bruise them in the best manner you can) : take a tammy or a fine cloth and rub them through till you have rubbed all the pulp out, and then put your soup in a clean pot with half a pint of spinach juice and boil it up for fifteen minutes; season with salt and a little pepper, then put it in your tureen with dice of bread toasted very hard.

Chilled Green Pea Soup

Ingredients

400g	Peas (frozen)		**30g**	Onion - chopped
300ml	Water		**Sprig**	Mint
300ml	Double Cream		**30g**	Butter

Method

1. Sweat the onion in the butter.
2. Add the peas and the water, bring to boil. Add the mint and season.
3. Cook for 40 minutes, add the cream, check seasoning and blend in a liquidizer.
4. Pass the soup through a fine strainer and chill.
5. Garnish with some cooked peas and a mint leaf.

This soup may be served hot or cold.

Chilled Cherry and Rose Soup

Ingredients

450g	Pitted Fresh Cherries	30g	Caster Sugar
175ml	Good Red Wine	1	Lemon - cut into slices
450ml	Water	1	Cinnamon Stick
Pinch	Ground Nutmeg	30g	Rose Petals
2tspn	Rosewater	1 tspn	Cornflour

Method

1. Boil all the ingredients except the cornflour for fifteen minutes.
2. Remove the cinnamon and the lemon.
3. Slacken the cornflour with a little cold water and whisk into the simmering soup.
4. Remove from heat and blend in a liquidizer and then pass through a fine sieve.
5. Check the seasoning and chill until required.
6. Garnish with some whipped cream or crème fraiche and a rose petal.

To Fricassee Soals White

Skin, wash and gut your soals very clean, cut off their heads, dry them in a cloth, then with your knife very carefully cut the flesh from the bones and fins on both sides; cut the flesh long ways then across so that each soal will be in eight pieces, take the heads and bones and put them into a sauce pan with a pint of water, a bundle of sweet herbs, an onion, a little whole pepper, two or three blades of mace, a little salt, a very little piece of lemon peel and a little crust of bread; cover it close, let it boil till half is wasted, then strain through a fine sieve, put it into a stew pan, put in the soals and half a pint of white wine a little parsley chopped fine, a few mushrooms cut small, a piece of butter as big as a hens egg rolled in flour, grate in a little nutmeg, set all together on the fire but keep shaking the pan all the while till the fish is enough. Then dish it up garnish with lemon.

Tian of Smoked Eel with Asparagus

Ingredients

400g	Smoked Eel	400g	Cooked New Potatoes - crushed
30g	Fine Diced Shallots	30g	Butter
Pinch	Ground Nutmeg	12 pieces	Cooked Asparagus
30ml	Lemon Juice	90ml	Olive Oil
1tspn	Chopped Chervil	100g	Mixed Lettuce Leaf
4	Pansy Flowers		

Method

1. Sweat the shallot and mix it with the potato, season with salt, pepper and nutmeg.
2. Mould in a 3 cm ring mould and tamp the potato down. Place on a greased baking sheet, brush with a little melted butter and cook in a hot oven until golden brown. Reserve and keep warm.
3. Slice the smoked eel and place on top of the potato and warm in the oven.
4. Reheat the asparagus in a little hot water and drain on kitchen paper.
5. Whisk the oil and lemon juice to an emulsion and mix in the chervil and season.
6. Arrange the potato and eel on a warm plate and place the asparagus around the potato. Place some lettuce leaf around the plate and dress with the olive oil dressing, garnish the plate with a pansy.

   This dish can be made with any smoked fish, salmon, mackerel or trout.

Fricassee of Sole with Mushrooms in a Saffron Cream

Ingredients

8	Fillets of Dover Sole - skins removed	30g	Finely Diced Shallot
120g	Sliced Oyster Mushrooms	30g	Salt Free Butter
Pinch	Saffron	100ml	White Wine
100ml	Fish Stock	150ml	Double Cream
200g	Puff Pastry		

Method

1. Roll out the puff paste ½ cm thick and cut into rectangles 10cm x 5 cm, egg wash and bake in a hot oven for 8 – 10 minutes, allow to cool when cooked.
2. Cut the sole into strips 5cm in length.
3. Sweat the shallot in the butter and then add the mushrooms.
4. Add the wine and reduce by half, add the stock and boil and season, add the saffron.
5. Reduce the stock by 2/3 and add the cream, check seasoning.
6. Reduce the cream by 2/3 and add the sole, cook for 4 – 5 minutes and remove from heat.
7. Split the pastry case and put on a plate, spoon some of the fish and sauce over the base pastry and place the lid on top. Brush the lid with a little melted butter.

Buttered Crab with Whisky and Ginger

Ingredients

400g	White Crab Meat ⁄ free of shell	**30g**	Shallot ⁄ finely diced
60g	Salt free Butter	**75ml**	Whisky
30g	Fresh Ginger ⁄ cut in fine strips	**60g**	Red Pepper ⁄ cut into fine strips
200ml	Double Cream	**Sprig**	Chervil

Method

1. Sweat the shallot and the ginger in the butter until soft.
2. Add the pepper and cook until soft.
3. Add the crab meat and heat through.
4. Add the whisky and flambé, add the cream and reduce by half.
5. Either serve on a warm plate on a pastry crust, or dressed back in the shell. Garnish with chervil.

Gratin of Plaice with Garlic and Shallot Marmalade

Ingredients

400g	Plaice Fillets - skins removed	80g	Button Mushrooms - sliced thinly
60g	Salt free Butter	100g	Grated Cheddar Cheese
1	Tomato - skinned, pips removed and chopped		
Pinch	Ground Ginger	4 tblsp	Double Cream
300g	Shallots peeled	10	Cloves of Garlic - peeled
60g	Brown Sugar	70ml	Madeira Wine
30ml	Olive Oil	Sprig	Parsley

Method

1. Line a buttered ramekin with 1 fillet and cut 1 fillet into strips for each portion. Mix the strips with the mushrooms, add the ginger and season and place into the centre of the fillet in the buttered ramekin.
2. Add the cream, cheese and some of the tomato, cover with some buttered foil.
3. Bake in a moderate oven for 10 minutes, then allow to rest.
4. Fry the shallots and garlic cloves in the olive oil until golden brown.
5. Add the sugar and allow to caramelize, then remove from heat and add the wine. Cook until it is of a thick jam like consistency.
6. Release the fish from the ramekin by running a small knife around the edge.
7. Drain on kitchen paper and place on a warm plate with some of the marmalade.
8. Garnish with picked parsley.

To Boile a Duck

Seeth the Duck with some good marrow bones or Mutton, and take the best of the broth, and put therein a few cloves, a good many sliced onions, and let them boile well together till the onions be tender, and then season your broth with vergious, and a little sugar and salt and a little brused pepper, take up your Duck and lay it upon sops and give it two slices upon the brest, and stick it ful of cloves and pour broth upon it.

Poached Breast of Duck with Quince and Lemon Confit

Ingredients

2	Barbary Duck Breasts		
500g	Quince ⁄ peeled and cored cut into ½ cm dice. Keep in water with some lemon juice		
100g	Caster Sugar	3	Lemons ⁄ peeled, pips removed & chopped
75ml	White Wine	500ml	Good Brown Stock
100ml	Madeira Wine	30g	Shallots ⁄ chopped
60g	Salt Free Butter	1tspn	Cornflour

To make the Confit

Method

1. Sweat the quince in half the butter and add the sugar, add the lemon and white wine and cook until the quince is soft and has the texture of thick jam.

Cooking The Duck

1. Sweat the shallot in a deep pan, add the Madeira and the stock and check the seasoning.
2. Remove the skin from the duck breast and reserve for garnish.
3. Place the duck in the stock and cook for 10 – 15 minutes, remove from stock and keep warm.
4. Cut the duck skin into thin strips and cook in olive oil until crisp and golden. Drain on kitchen paper.
5. Reduce the cooking liquor by 2/3 and slacken the cornflour with a little water, whisk into the simmering stock. When it thickens check the seasoning and pour through a fine strainer into a sauce boat.
6. Slice the duck breast at an angle not too thin and divide between two plates.
7. Arrange some of the confit on the duck and top with some crisp duck skin.
8. Pour the sauce around the duck and garnish with fresh herbs.

Chicken Pie

Ingredients

Hot Water Pastry

250g	Strong Flour (Bread Flour)	125g	Butter
125ml	Water	Pinch	Salt

Filling

200g	Chicken Breast - free of bone and skin		
200g	Chicken Leg - meat diced		
500g	Streaky Bacon - rind removed		
50ml	Chicken Stock	3 Sheets	Leaf Gelatine - soaked in cold water

Method for the Pastry

1. Boil the water and salt and butter together.
2. Add to the flour and stir until the paste comes together and leaves the sides of the pan.
3. Cool.
4. Line a well greased pie mould or deep flan tin.

Method for the Filling

5. Wrap the chicken breast in the bacon.
6. Place half of the pieces of chicken leg in the pie base and pour in half of the cold chicken stock.
7. Place the wrapped breast on top and cover with the remainder of the diced chicken. Place the soaked and drained gelatine on top of the chicken.
8. Egg wash the top of the pastry base and roll out the remaining paste for a lid, cover the pie and crimp the top.
9. Cut a hole in the centre of the lid to allow steam out and egg wash the lid.
10. Bake at 160oC for an hour, then drop the temperature to 140oC for an hour.
12. When cooked cool and remove from the mould.

Fillet of Lamb with Rosemary and Creamed Leeks

Ingredients

2	Best ends of Lamb - eye of meat removed from bone and fat		
10g	Rosemary	60g	Butter
250g	Minced Chicken	2	Eggs
200ml	Double Cream	Pinch	Ground Nutmeg
60g	Shallot Chopped	75ml	Red Wine
200ml	Brown Stock	200g	Leeks - cut into strips

Method

1. Remove the eye of meat from the best end and seal in a little oil, season and dry on kitchen paper.
2. Blend the chicken in a food processor and season with salt, pepper and nutmeg.
3. Add the eggs one at a time blending thoroughly.
4. Gradually add the cream and tarragon. Check seasoning.
5. Spread some cling film on your work surface and spead some of the chicken mix in the centre, place half of a lamb fillet on top and cover with chicken mix.
6. Roll up the cling film and tie at each end. Refrigerate until required.
7. Sweat the leeks in butter until soft, season and add the cream.
8. Simmer until the cream is well reduced and thick, check the seasoning.
9. Sweat the shallot in a little butter, add the wine and reduce by half. Check the seasoning. Add half of the rosemary.
10. Add the stock and reduce by half, if the sauce is thin thicken it with some cornflour.
11. Fill a deep saucepan with water, bring to boil and place in the lamb. Cook for 15 – 20 minutes, remove from water and allow to rest for 10 minutes.
12. Place leeks on centre of the plate, unwrap the lamb, drain and slice as required placing the slices on the leeks.
13. Strain the sauce through a fine strainer and pour around the dish.
14. Garnish with a little rosemary.

Vegetables available in the Summer Season

Asparagus, Lettuce, New Potatoes, Cauliflower, Broccoli, Globe Artichokes, Cabbage, Spinach, Carrots, Turnips, Peas, Beans, Fennel, Celery, Sorrel, Onions, Shallots, Oyster Plant, Beetroots.

Recipes and suggestions may be found in the Vegetable and Salad Section.

To Make Fine Cheesecakes

Take a pint of cream, warm it and put to it five quarts of milk warm from the cow, then put runnet to it, and give it a stir about; and when it is come, put the curd in a linen bag or cloth, let it drain well away from the whey, but do not squeeze it much; then put it in a mortar, and break the curd as fine as butter; put to your curd half a pound of sweet almonds blanched and beat exceedingly fine, and half a pound of macaroons beat very fine: then add to it the yolks of nine eggs beaten, a whole nutmeg grated two perfumed plums, dissolved in with rose or orange water, ha'f a pound of fine sugar; mix all well together, then melt a pound and a quarter of butter and stir it well in it, and half a pound of currants plumped, to let stand to cool till you use it; then make your puff paste, you may leave out the currants, for change nor nerd you put in the perfumed plums if you dislike them; you may put in as much tincture of saffron as will give them a high colour, but no currants: this we call saffron cheesecakes; the other without currants, almond cheesecakes with currants fine cheesecakes.

Lemon Possett and Summer Berries

Ingredients

Possett

500ml	Double Cream	150g	Caster Sugar
2	Lemons ⁄ Juice and zest cut into thin strips. Cook the zest in a little water and sugar.		

Berries & Coulis

100g	Strawberries	100g	Raspberries
50g	Blackberries	4 branches	Redcurrants
90g	Caster Sugar	50ml	Water

Method

Possett

1. Boil the cream, the sugar and lemon juice for exactly 3 minutes and then pour into a bowl or moulds. Set in the fridge for as long as possible.

Coulis

1. Take half of the strawberries and half of the raspberries add the sugar and water and bring to the boil, blend in a liquidizer and pass through a fine strainer into a sauce boat. Allow to cool.

Arranging the dish

1. Scoop a portion of possett onto a plate or turn out of the mould.
2. Arrange a mixture of berries around the plate and drizzle with the coulis.
3. Dust with icing sugar and decorate with the zest and a mint leaf.

31

Strawberry and Lavender Jelly

Ingredients

300g	Strawberries – thinly sliced	**50g**	Caster Sugar
4 sheets	Leaf Gelatine – soaked & when soft squeeze all water out		
500ml	Sparkling Wine	**400ml**	Double Cream
30g	Icing Sugar	**3 drops**	Vanilla Extract
1 Sprig	Lavender		

Method

1. Place the strawberries and the sugar in a bowl just cover with some of the wine.
2. Put the bowl over a pan of hot water for about an hour with the sprig of lavender.
3. Strain the juice and wine through a wet piece of muslin into a clean pan. Reserve the strawberries but discard the lavender.
4. Warm the juice and dissolve the soaked gelatine in it. Pass again into a clean bowl.
5. Add the rest of the wine and allow to start to set, pour into glasses or dish and chill in the fridge.
6. Whisk the cream and icing sugar and vanilla to peak, pipe or spoon on to top of set jelly. Top with some of the sliced strawberries.
7. Alternatively turn out from the dish and cut into shapes with a warm cutter or knife and arrange on a plate.

Almond Ice Cream with a Compote of Cherries

Ingredients

500ml	Whipping Cream	250g	Icing Sugar
50ml	Ameretto Liqueur	30g	Ground Almonds
500g	Pitted Cherries	39g	Salt free Butter
60g	Caster Sugar	50ml	Cherry Brandy

Method

1. Whisk the cream, icing sugar, almonds and Ameretto to just under peak.
2. Place the mixture in a clean bowl and cover with cling film allow to set in the freezer overnight.
3. In a frying pan heat the cherries in the butter.
4. Add the sugar and mix in well.
5. Flame with the cherry brandy and serve with a scoop or two of the almond ice cream.

"Beauteous springs to yellow Autumn turn'd."

— Sonnet #104

In his writing on this teeming and bountiful season, Shakespeare reveals his understanding of nature, and his rural, Warwickshire upbringing:

> Earth's increase, harvest plenty
> Barns and garners never empty;
> Vines with clust'ring bunches growing,
> Plants with goodly burthen bowing;
> All come to you at the farthest
> In the very end of the harvest!
>
> *- The Tempest*

This time of Harvest, thanksgiving, solemnity and reflection was not without fun and frivolity. The vigil of All Saint's Day, "All Hallow Even," or, "Hallow Even," the predecessor to our modern "Halloween," was a night of great festivity. Many of our modern traditions, such as diving for apples and roasting nuts upon the fire were popular pastimes on All Hallow Even. Like our modern Halloween, this was a time of goblins, fairies, and sprites, however, as John Gay's poem, "Spell" reminds us, the most potent magic in the air was love:

> Two hazel nuts I threw into the flame,
> And to each nut I gave a sweet-heart's name:
> This with the loudest bounce me sore amaz'd,
> That in a flame of brightest colour blaz'd;
> As blaz'd the nut, so may thy passion grow,
> For t'was thy nut that did so brightly glow!

These shortened, darker, autumnal days drew family and friends together around the warming heat of blazing bonfires, or the steamy kitchen hearth. Shakespeare's delightful comedy *Merry Wives of Windsor* captures the mischief and playfulness of this season.

Merry Wives of Windsor is the one Shakespeare play that is focused exclusively on the everyday lives of ordinary, middle class, Elizabethan folk. The play's principal characters are the quick-witted Mistress Page and Mistress Ford. The play also features one of Shakespeare's greatest comic characters, Sir John Falstaff. Falstaff, in pursuit of money, first deceives the wives. The wives uncover Falstaff's treachery and enact a swift deception and comic revenge upon him. In true Shakespearean form, truth and love triumph in the end. *Merry Wives of Windsor* also reminds us of the wonderfully filling foods that comfort us against the season's brisk chill:

"Come, we have a hot venison pasty to dinner!"

... says Mistress Page. Likewise, the recipes in this chapter are intending to soothe you and yours on crisp Autumn days.

Celebrations in Autumn

Autumn starts in September, and is the transitional season from the warmth of summer to the cold of winter. Before the 16th century this season was referred to as "harvest" and gradually, as people moved from working on the land to getting work in the towns, the word harvest became associated only with the gathering in of food and reaping of crops for the winter months.

The term "fall" was used in German and Old English languages as a metaphor for the Autumn season and was associated with the falling of the leaves or the fall of the year. The term was taken to the New World by the 16th century settlers and is still in use there today. Our word Autumn comes from the Latin "autumnus".

St. Martin's Summer was the term used to describe the late hot weather on St. Martin's Day, November 11th, when summer was supposed to end. This was the most widely used term until " Indian Summer" was introduced from the USA in the 20th Century.

St. Luke's Summer, 18th October, was an alternative to St. Martin's Summer and yet another alternative was "All Hallow Summer" as Halloween falls on October 31st. The term "All Hallow Summer" is used in Shakespeare's *King Henry 1V,* Part 1, Act 1, Scene 2.

Today the word Autumn conjures up the images of welcoming log fires, succulent orchard fruits and berries, beautiful colours - the russets, reds and gold of leaves, the hazy sunny days and chilly nights. Festivals have always been a part of this season with the Harvest, Halloween and the Autumnal Equinox. Wheat sheaves were offered to the gods in the form of corn dollies and were later adopted by the Christians as harvest sheaves of bread, baked in the shape of wheat. There has been dancing and singing, eating and drinking to celebrate the Harvest, which would keep us in food throughout the long, cold winter months.

Foods prepared at this time would include: apples, plums, root vegetables, breads, pork and mutton. The dishes selected for this section have all been influenced by the reasons given above. The commodities used are the same as those available to the Elizabethans - they are a reflection of Autumn and our Heritage.

The FOOD of LOVE

The Taste of Shakespeare in Four Seasons

Autumn Season Index

Rules to be Observed in Making Soups and Broths

First take great care the pots or saucepans and covers be very clean and free from all grease and sand, and that they be well tinned for fear of giving the broths or soups any brassy taste. If you have time to stew as softly as possible, it will both have a finer flavour and the meat will be tenderer; but then observe, when you make soups or broths for present use, it is to be done softly, do not put much more water than you intend to have for soup or broth; and if you have the convenience of an earthen pan or pipkin, set it on wood embers till it boils, then skim it and put in your seasoning; cover it close and set it on embers, so that it may do very softly for some time, and both the meat and broth will be delicious. You must observe in all broths and soups that one thing does not taste more than another, but that the taste be equal, and that it has a fine agreeable relish, according to what you design it for, and you must be sure all the greens and herbs you put in be cleaned, washed and picked.

To Make White Barley Pottage

First make your stock with an old hen, a knuckle of veal, a scrag end of mutton, some spice, sweet herbs and onions; boil together till it be strong enough, then have your barley ready boiled very tender and white, strain some of it through a cullender; have your bread ready toasted in your dish, with some fine green herbs minced chervil, spinach, sorrel and put in your dish with some broth to your bread then the barley strained and re strained.

Barley Pottage

Ingredients

1 ltr	Chicken Stock	60g	Pearl Barley ‑ cooked
30g	Sorrel ‑ finely shredded	60g	Spinach ‑ finely shredded
60g	Gem Lettuce ‑ finely shredded	60	Chopped Onions
100g	Chopped Potato	4g	Chopped Chervil
4g	Chopped Parsley	30g	Salt Free Butter

Method

1. Cook the barley and cool quickly.
2. Sweat the onion in the butter and add the sorrel, lettuce and the spinach. Cook until wilted.
3. Add the stock and bring to boil, add the potato.
4. Bring to boil and season, cook for 30 minutes.
5. Blend the soup in a liquidizer and return to a clean pan, re‑boil and check seasoning, add the herbs and barley.
6. Cook for 5 minutes and serve.

Almond and Chicken Velouté

Ingredients

100g	Chicken Breast - skin and bones removed		
1 ltr	Chicken Stock		
60g	Onion - chopped	30g	Leek - white only
100g	Ground Almonds	30g	Salt free Butter
30g	Flour	100ml	Cream
20g	Flaked Almonds - toasted.		

Method

1. Sweat the onion and leek in the butter.
2. Add the flour and mix, cook for 3 – 4 minutes stirring constantly.
3. Gradually add the stock stirring gently.
4. Bring to boil check seasoning and add the almonds.
5. Place chicken in the soup and cook for 30 minutes.
6. Remove chicken and cool, cut into thin strips.
7. Blend the rest of the soup in a liquidizer and then pass through a fine strainer, return to the pan and re-boil, add the cream and check seasoning.
8. Add chicken and flaked almonds and serve.

Amulet of Artichokes and Beans

Ingredients

200g	Artichoke bottoms - cooked and cut into quarters		
150g	Broad Beans - blanched and skin removed		
60g	Shallot	1	Clove Garlic - finely chopped
30g	Butter	60g	Sorrel shredded
50ml	White Wine	150ml	Double Cream
2	Egg yolks	10g	Chervil chopped
10g	Tarragon - chopped	Pinch	Nutmeg
200g	Puff Pastry - cut into rounds and bake in a hot oven for 10 minutes		
4 Slices	Truffle or Black Olive		

Method

1. Sweat the onion and garlic in the butter and then add the beans and artichokes.
2. Season and add the wine and reduce by 1/3. Add the sorrel.
3. Add 2/3 of the cream and check seasoning. Cook for 15 minutes, gently simmering.
4. When the cream has reduced to a coating consistency, whisk the egg yolks and the remainder of the cream together and add some of the hot mixture to the cold cream. Then stir into the rest of the vegetable mixture. Do not allow to boil, just reheat and thicken.
5. Add the chopped tarragon and chervil and serve on the pastry base. Sprinkle with nutmeg.
6. Place in the pastry case, brush the lid with the melted butter and dress with the truffle.

To Ragoo Oysters

Take a quart of the largest oysters you can get, open them, save the liquor and strain through a fine sieve; wash your oysters in warm water; make a batter thus: take two yolks of egg, beat them well, grate in half a nutmeg, cut a little lemon peel small, a good deal of parsley, a spoonful of juice of spinage, two spoonfuls of cream or milk, beat it up with flour to a thick batter; have ready some butter in a stew pan, dip your oysters one by one into the batter and have ready crumbs of bread then roll them in it and fry them quickly and brown, some with the bread and some without, take them out of the pan and set them before the fire, then have ready a quart of chestnuts shelled and skinned, fry them in butter; when they are enough take them up, pour the fat out of the pan, shake a little flour all over the pan and rub a piece of butter the size of a hens egg all over the pan till it is melted and thick, then put in the oyster liquor, three or four blades of mace, stir it round, put in a few pistachio nuts shelled, let them boil, then put in the chestnuts and half a pint of wine, lay the oysters in a dish pour the ragoo over them.

Scallops and Jerusalem Artichokes in a Saffron Sauce

Ingredients

20	Scallops ⁄ removed from shell, nut only no roe		
150g	Jerusalem Artichokes ⁄ peeled & thinly sliced		
30g	Finely Diced Shallot	30g	Salt Free Butter
Pinch	Saffron	50ml	White Wine
150ml	Double Cream		

Method

1. Quickly fry the scallops in the butter and remove to a plate, keep warm.
2. Fry the artichokes in the butter and add the shallot. Add the wine and reduce by half.
3. Add the cream, boil and check seasoning. Add the saffron and cook for 5 minutes.
4. When the cream has reduced by half check seasoning, place scallops back into sauce and reheat for 2 – 3 minutes.
5. Serve with some braised rice.

Fillet of Cod with Smoked Oyster Fricassée

Ingredients

4 ⁄ 125g Slices of Cod ⁄ all skin & bones removed.

8	Smoked Oysters	150ml	White wine
30g	Shallots ⁄ chopped	60g	Button Mushrooms ⁄ cut in ¼
30g	Salt Free Butter	30ml	Olive oil
150ml	Double Cream	4 sprigs	Chervil
100g	Tomatoes ⁄ blanched, pips removed &diced		

Method

1. Dip the cod through some seasoned flour and fry in the butter and oil until golden brown on each side.
2. When cooked remove from pan and keep warm.
3. Add the shallots to the pan and cook for 2 minutes. Add the mushrooms and cook for 2 minutes, season and add the wine, reduce by 2/3.
4. Add the oysters and the cream and cook until the cream has reduced by ½ . Check seasoning.
5. Add the tomatoes and heat through.
6. Place some of the fricassee on a plate, place a piece of cod on top and garnish with chervil.

Potted Salmon with Green Peppercorns and Lobster Sauce

Ingredients

500g	Salmon - free of skin and bone, cut in strips		
5g	Green Peppercorns	30g	Shallot - finely diced
80ml	Double Cream	30g	Butter
30g	Chopped Onion	200g	Chopped Lobster Shell
30g	Chopped Celery	30g	Chopped Carrot
Sprig	Tarragon	60g	Tomato Paste
30g	Butter	30ml	Brandy
60ml	Double Cream	200ml	Fish Stock

Method

The Salmon

1. Fry the salmon quickly in the butter, add the shallot and peppercorns.
2. Add the cream and boil, check seasoning.
3. Cook until the cream is well reduced. Pour mixture into a greased ramekin and keep warm.

The Lobster Sauce

1. Fry the shell in the butter, add the vegetables and then the tomato paste. Cook for 5 minutes - stirring.
2. Add the brandy and flambé, add the stock and boil, check seasoning, add half the tarragon, cook for 30 minutes.
3. Add cream and reduce by 2/3.
4. Pass sauce through a fine strainer, if not thick enough reduce further.

Assembling the dish

1. Reheat the salmon, press firmly with a spoon and turn out onto a plate.
2. Pour some lobster sauce around the salmon, garnish with some tarragon.

To Make Fine Patties

Slice either turkey, lamb or chicken, with an equal quantity of the fat of lamb, loin of veal or the inside of a loin of beef, a little parsley, thyme and lemon peel shred, put it all in a marble mortar and pound it very fine, season it with white pepper and salt, then make a fine puff paste, roll it out in thin square sheets, put the forcemeat in the middle, cover it over, close them all around, and cut the paste even: just before they go into the oven wash them over with the yolk of an egg, and bake them twenty minutes in a quick oven; have ready a little white gravy seasoned with pepper, salt, and a little shallot, thickened up with a little cream or butter; as soon as the patties come out of the oven, make a hole in the top and pour in some gravy; you must take care not to put too much gravy in, for fear of its running out at the sides, and spoiling the patties.

Chicken Patties with a Herb Sauce

Ingredients

Patties:

2	Chicken Breasts - cut in half	60g	Shallots - chopped fine
60g	Button Mushrooms - chopped small		
2	Egg yolks }		
Pinch	Salt } Egg Wash - whisk together.		

Sauce:

1 Sprig	Chervil	4	Smoked Bacon Rashers
1 Sprig	Parsley	1 Sprig	Tarragon
200ml	Cream	30g	Butter
30g	Shallot - chopped fine	60ml	White Wine
600gms	Puff Pastry		

Method

1. Roll out the pastry ¼ cm thick, cut circles of paste 14cm and 10 cm for each patty.
2. Sweat the shallot and the mushrooms in the butter and season well, allow to cool.
3. Seal the chicken in a frying pan in a little oil, season and remove from pan. Cut each breast into two pieces.
4. Wrap each piece of chicken in the bacon.
5. Lay the smaller of the pastry circles on a greased baking tray and egg wash the edges.
6. Place some of the mushroom and shallot mixture in the centre of the pastry and place a piece of chicken on top.
7. Cover with the larger of the pastry circles and crimp the edges together. Make three slits with a small sharp knife in the centre of the pastry. Egg wash.
8. Bake in a hot oven for 15 – 20 minutes, remove from oven and keep warm.

The Sauce & Dish Assembly

1. Sweat the shallot in the butter, add the wine and reduce by ½ .
2. Add the cream and boil, check seasoning and add the herbs.
3. Reduce by ½ .
4. Place patty on plate, cut in half, open and pour sauce into centre.

Haricot of Mutton

Ingredients

400g	Diced Mutton or Lamb	**2**	Crushed Cloves Garlic
100g	Alsace Bacon - cut into lardoons	**12**	Button Onions
200g	Cooked Haricot Beans (tinned are fine)	**1ltr** Good Brown Stock	
30g	Tomato Puree	**30g**	Salt Free Butter
100ml	White Wine	**Sprig**	Parsley

Method

1. Quickly fry the bacon in the butter, add the onions and garlic and colour.
2. Add the mutton and seal, add the tomato paste and then the wine, reduce the wine by ½ .
3. Boil and season. Cook for 1 hour, check the meat for tenderness, if cooked, thicken the liquor with the slackened cornflour.
4. Add the drained beans and cook for further 30 minutes.
5. Serve with creamed potatoes and garnish with the parsley.

Noisettes of Venison with Pippins and Brambles

Ingredients

600g	Loin of Venison - off the bone & fat trimmed.	30g	Shallot - chopped
100g	Blackberries	1	Apple (Cox's Orange Pippin)
60g	Salt Free Butter	30g	Brown Sugar
60ml	Cassis Liqueur	60ml	Red Wine
500ml	Good Brown Stock	1 tspn	Cornflour
Sprig	Chervil	10ml	Oil

Method

1. Cut the loin into 8 mini steaks, reserve in the fridge until required.
2. Slice the apple in 2cm slices and then into batons.
3. With a sharp knife remove the corners of the apple batons in an arc, shaping the apples into a elongated barrel shape, keep all the apple trimmings for the sauce.
4. Sweat the shallot in half the butter and then add half the blackberries and the apple trimmings.
5. Add the cassis and wine and reduce by ½ .
6. Add the stock and reduce by 2/3.
7. Fry the apples in the remaining butter and add the sugar. Cook quickly until they are caramelised, remove from heat and cool down.
8. Blend the sauce in a liquidizer and pass through a fine strainer, return to pan and re-boil. Check seasoning and thicken with the cornflour.
9. Fry the venison in the oil and add a little butter. Season and cook to desired degree of cooking. Remove from pan and drain on kitchen paper, place on plate, garnish with apples and remaining blackberries and pour sauce around venison. Garnish with chervil.

To Make a Venison Pasty

Instructions

Take a Peck of fine Flower, and three Pounds of fresh Butter, break your Butter into your Flower, and put in one Egg, and make it into a Past with so much cold cream as you think fit, but do not mould it too much, then roul it pretty thin and broad, almost square, then lay some Butter on the bottom, then season your Venison on the fleshy side with Pepper grosly beaten, and Salt mixed, then lay your Venison upon your butter with the seasoned side downward, and then cut the Venison over with your Knife quite cross the Pasty to let the Gravie come out the better in baking, then rub some seasoning in those Cuts, and do not lay any else because it will make it look ill-favoured and black, then put some paste rouled thin about the Meat to keep it in compass, and lay Butter on the top, then close it up and bake it very well, but you must trim it up with several Fancies made in the same Paste, and make also a Tunnel or Vent, and just when you are going to set it into the Oven, put in half a Pint of Clarret Wine, that will season your Venison finely, and make it shall not look or taste greasie, thus you may bake Mutton if you please.

Venison Pasty

Ingredients

500g	Fillet of Venison Loin - free of bone & skin		
200g	Button Mushrooms - finely chopped		
100g	Shallot - finely chopped	**2 cloves**	Crushed Garlic
60g	Butter	500g	Puff Pastry
1	Egg - for egg wash	1	Sprig Rubbed Rosemary
Pinch	Nutmeg	100ml	Red Wine

Pancake batter

120g	Flour	1	Egg
300ml	Milk		Seasoning

Method

1. Mix the flour, egg and seasoning together to a batter and make 3 large pancakes.
2. Make the pancakes as large as possible and thinly.
3. Sweat the shallot and garlic in the butter and add the mushrooms and wine. Cook for 6 minutes and add the rosemary and nutmeg. Season and allow to cool.
4. Roll out the pastry into a rectangle.
5. Cover the rectangle with the pancakes.
6. Seal the venison very quickly in a little oil and season well.
7. Spread the mushroom mixture over the pancake and place the venison on top.
8. Wrap the pastry over the venison and seal with egg wash.
9. Place onto a greased baking sheet with the seam at the bottom.
10. Egg wash the pasty and cut a hole in the centre to allow the steam to escape.
11. Bake in a moderate oven for 30 – 40 minutes.

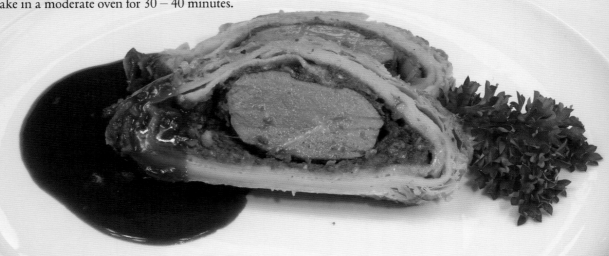

How to Make a Good Marchpaine.

First take a pound of long smal almonds and blanch them in cold water, and dry them as drye as you can, then grinde them small, and put no licour to them but as you must needs to keepe them from boyling, and that licour that you put in must be rosewater, in manner as you shall think good, but wet your Pestel therin, when ye have beaten them fine, take halfe a pound of Sugar and more, and see that it be beaten small in pouder, it must be fine sugar, then put it to your Almonds and beate them altogither, when they be beaten, take your wafers and cut them compasse round, and of the bignes you will have your Marchpaine, and then as soone as you can after the tempering of your stuffe, let it be put in your paste, and strike it abroad with a flat stick as even as you can, and pinch the very stuffe as it were an edge set upon, and then put a paper under it, and set it upon a faire boord, and lay lattin Basin over it the bottome upwarde, and then lay burning coles upon the bottom of the basin. To see how it baketh, if it happen to bren too fast in some place, folde papers as broad as the place is. Lay it upon that place, and thus with attending ye shal bake it a little more then a quarter of an houre, and when it is wel baked, put on your gold and biskets, and stick in Comfits, and so you shall make a good Marchpaine. Or ever that you bake it you must cast on it fine Sugar and Rosewater that will make it look like Ice.

Marzipan Tartlets with Spiced Orange and Plums

Ingredients
Almond Paste

125g	Butter	1	Whole Egg
60g	Ground Almonds	3 Drops	Almond Essence
200g	Flour	Pinch	Salt
100g	Icing Sugar		

Method Almond Pastry

1. In a food processor blend the butter and icing sugar
2. Add the egg and a little flour and blend.
3. Add the rest of the ingredients and blend all together.
4. Rest for at least 1 hour.
5. Line the tartlet moulds with the paste. Line with the greaseproof paper or foil and fill with beans. Rest for 30 minutes in the fridge.
6. Bake blind at 170oC in a pre-heated oven for 10 minutes.
7. Cool and remove pastry cases from mould.
8. Fill with mousse and chill.

Orange Mousse

350ml	Whipping Cream	1	Orange - zest and juice only
80g	Caster Sugar	Pinch	Ground Ginger
Pinch	Cinnamon	Pinch	Allspice
4	Egg Yolks	3.5 Sheets	Gelatine - soaked in cold water until soft

Method for the Mousse

1. Boil half the cream. Whisk the egg yolks with the sugar and spices.
2. Remove the cream from heat and whisk onto egg yolks. Reheat stirring constantly until the mix coats the back of the spoon.
3. Add the gelatine and cool. Strain and add the orange juice and zest.
4. Whip the remaining cream and fold it into the cold orange mousse mixture.
5. Line 4 tartlet moulds with the marzipan paste and place some foil in each and bake blind. When cooked, remove the foil and place the cooled marzipan tartlets onto a wire cooling rack.
6. Fill with the orange mousse and allow to set in a cool place.

Plum Confit

Ingredients

500g	Plums - cut in half stones removed	150g	Brown Sugar
60ml	Prunelle or Red Wine	Pinch	Cinnamon
1	Bay Leaf	Pinch	Ginger

Method

1. Boil sugar, wine and spices together to a syrup and place in the plums. Cook for 10 minutes and cool down, chill before placing some of the plums on top of orange mousse and drizzle with the syrup.

Orange Flower Custard

Ingredients

400ml	Whipping Cream	100g	Caster Sugar
30ml	Orange Flower Water	150ml	Orange Juice
Zest	of 1 Orange	Pinch	Ginger
5	Eggs		

Method

1. Whisk the cream, eggs, orange juice, sugar and ginger together.
2. Strain into a bowl and add the zest.
3. Pour into greased ramekins and bake until set in a water bath in the oven.
4. When cooked chill well before turning out of the ramekins.
5. To serve, place on a dish and dress with any poached fruit such as plums, pears or blackberries.
6. Garnish with a mint leaf.

Poached Spiced Pears in Red Wine

Ingredients

4	Pears - peeled whole, cored & the stalk intact
150g	Caster Sugar
500ml	Red Wine
2g	Ground Ginger
1	Bay Leaf
200ml	Orange Juice

200ml	Water
1	Cinnamon Stick
1	Orange - studded with cloves

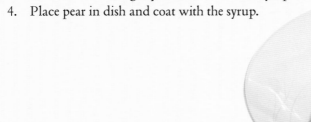

Method

1. Boil all the ingredients together, add the pears and cook until the pears are a deep red colour.
2. Remove pears from the liquid and cool in the fridge.
3. Reduce the cooking liquor until thick and syrup like.
4. Place pear in dish and coat with the syrup.

To Make a Pumpion Pye

Instructions

Take about halfe a pound of Pumpion and slice it, a handfull of Tyme, a little Rosemary, Parsley and sweet Marjoram slipped off the stalks, and chop them smal, then take Cinamon, Nutmeg, Pepper, and six Cloves, and beat them; take ten Eggs and beat them; then mix them, and beat them altogether, and put in as much Sugar as you think fit, then fry them like a froiz; after it is fryed, let it stand till it be cold, then fill your Pye, take sliced Apples thinne round wayes, and lay a row of the Froiz, and a layer of Apples with Currans betwixt the layer while your Pye is fitted, and put in a good deal of sweet butter before you close it; when the Pye is baked, take six yolks of Eggs, some white-wine or Verjuyce, and make a Caudle of this, but not too thick; cut up the Lid and put it in, stir them well together whilst the Eggs and Pumpions be not perceived, and so serve it up.

"We'll use this watery pumpion; we'll teach him to know turtles from jays."

— Mistress Ford, *Merry Wives of Windsor*

Pumpkin Pie

Ingredients

400g	Pumpkin - cut in ½ cm dice		150g	Apple - cut in ½ cm dice
60g	Butter		175g	Caster Sugar
90g	Currants		1 Sprig	Thyme - rubbed from stalk & chopped
1 Sprig	Marjoram - picked and chopped		1 Sprig	Rosemary - rubbed from stalk & chopped
Pinch	Ground Nutmeg		Pinch	Cinnamon
Pinch	Ground Ginger		Pinch	Ground Cloves
5	Eggs		400ml	Double Cream
400g	Sweet Pastry			

Method

1. Line a greased 8 inch flan ring on a greased baking sheet and rest in the fridge.
2. Fry the pumpkin in the butter until soft. Add the apple and cook for 8 minutes. Then add the sugar, spices and herbs. Cool.
3. Beat the eggs and cream together and add the pumpkin mix. Check the seasoning.
4. Fill the flan base with the pumpkin mix, sprinkle with cinnamon and bake in a moderate oven for 40 minutes until light brown and set.
5. Remove from oven and cool before removing flan ring.

Harvest Supper
Menu

Spiced Parsnip and Apple Soup

———

Pike Pudding with Oyster Sauce

———

Roast Capon with
Sausages and Sage and Onion Dressing
Roast Potatoes
Carrots in Honey and Orange Glaze
Fried Green Beans and Garlic

———

Damson and Rhubarb Pie
Scalded Cream

———

Mulled Cyder

Spiced Parsnip and Apple Soup

Ingredients

500g	Parsnips - peeled and diced		200g	Apple Peeled - cored and diced
5g	Ground Coriander		5g	Ground Cumin
60g	Salt Free Butter		100g	Chopped Onion
5g	Turmeric		5g	Ground Ginger
1ltr	Vegetable Stock		150ml	Double Cream
2	Cloves Garlic - crushed		1 Sprig	Coriander - chopped

Method

1. Sweat the onion and garlic in the butter, add the spices and mix well.
2. Add the parsnip and apples and then the stock.
3. Bring to the boil and check the seasoning, boil for 40 minutes and blend in a liquidizer. Pass through a fine strainer into the clean pan and re-boil.
4. Add the cream and heat through, garnish with the chopped coriander.

Pike Pudding with Oyster Sauce

Ingredients

Pudding

500g	Pike - free of skin and bone, diced up		
3	Eggs	400ml	Double Cream
Pinch	Nutmeg	Pinch	Ginger
Pinch	Mace	150g	White Breadcrumbs - soaked in milk

Oyster sauce

4	Oysters - out of shell in their juice	30g	Shallots - chopped fine
30g	Salt Free Butter	100ml	White Wine
200ml	Double Cream		

Method

The Pudding

1. Make sure the fish and cream are very cold.
2. In a food processor blend the fish to a paste. Add salt, pepper and spices and blend again.
3. Gradually blend in the eggs, 1 at a time. Add the breadcrumbs and blend.
4. Gradually blend in the cream, check seasoning.
5. Remove into a clean bowl and place in the fridge.
6. Grease four small pudding basins and fill with the fish mixture. Cover with cling film and place the basins in a hot water bath. Cook in the oven for 10 – 15 minutes, the pudding will feel firm. Allow to rest.

The Oyster Sauce

1. Sweat the shallot in the butter, add the wine and reduce by ½.
2. Add the oysters and the cream, season and cook until the cream has reduced by 2/3.
3. Blend in a liquidizer and pass through a fine strainer and keep it hot.

Assembling the dish

1. Turn the pudding out onto kitchen paper to drain.
2. Place on a warm plate and pour the sauce over the pudding.
3. Garnish with some dill.

Roast Capon with Sausages and Sage and Onion Dressing

Ingredients

1	2kg Capon	500g	Chipolata Sausages
250g	Streaky Bacon - rind removed	400ml	Chicken Stock
1tspn	Cornflour	90g	Goose or Duck Fat
400g	White Breadcrumbs.	100g	Onion - finely diced
25g	Chopped Sage	10g	Chopped Parsley
60g	Butter	75ml	Chicken Stock
Pinch	Nutmeg	Pinch	Mace

1. Sweat the onion in the butter. 2. Add the breadcrumbs and herbs. 3. Season and add the boiling stock Allow the mixture to thicken.

Method

1. Remove the wishbone from the capon, fill some of the neck cavity with some of the sage and onion mix. Make the rest of the mixture into balls and bake in the oven
2. Season the capon inside and out. Truss the capon.
3. Roast in the goose fat in a moderate oven, basting frequently - allow 20 minutes per 500g.
4. Roll the chipolatas in the bacon and bake them in the oven.
5. When the capon is cooked allow it to rest for ½ hour.
6. Pour off the excess fat and heat the roasting tray on the stove. Add the chicken stock and season. Reduce by 2/3 and thicken with the cornflour and pass through a fine strainer.
7. Carve the capon giving some breast meat and some leg meat per portion.
8. Garnish with the sausages and sage and onion balls and pour the gravy over the meat.

Serves 6 - 8 people

Carrots Glazed in Honey and Orange

Ingredients

500g	Carrots – cut into batons	60g	Clear Honey
75ml	Orange Juice	30g	Butter
1 Sprig	Parsley – chopped		

Method

1. Cover the carrots in the orange juice and the honey, if not covered add a little water. Add the butter, season and cook with a lid on the pan.
2. When boiling rapidly, remove the lid and allow the liqor to reduce forming a glaze. When the carrots are coated in the glaze, sprinkle them with the chopped parsley.

Fried Green Beans

Ingredients

400g	Green Beans	60g	Butter
Pinch	Nutmeg		

Method

1. Pre-cook some beans in boiling salted water – do not over cook. Refresh in cold water and drain on kitchen paper.
2. Melt the butter in a frying pan and place in the beans and cook for 5 – 6 minutes. Season and add the nutmeg.
3. Drain before serving.

Damson and Rhubarb Pie with Scalded Cream

Ingredients

400g	Stoned Damsons	300g	Rhubarb
60g	Butter	150g	Caster Sugar
2g	Ground Ginger	Pinch	Ground Mace
50ml	Orange Juice	400g	Puff Pastry
1	Egg - for egg wash		

Method

1. Cook the damsons and the rhubarb in the butter for 6 – 8 minutes.
2. Add the sugar, spices and the orange juice. Cool.
3. Grease a large pie dish and place the damson mix into it.
4. Cover with the puff pastry and egg wash the lid. Make 3 – 4 slits with a small knife in the centre of the lid and dust with some caster sugar.
5. Bake in a moderate oven until golden brown.

Scalded Cream

Ingredients

500ml	Double Cream	200g	Caster Sugar
4	Drops Vanilla Extract		

Method

1. Boil the cream, sugar and vanilla for 3 minutes and pour into a clean bowl and allow to set in the fridge,

   It is best to prepare this cream the day before it is required.

Mulled Cyder

Ingredients

1 ltr	Cider	1 ltr	Apple Juice
1	Orange - studded with Cloves	1	Cinnamon Stick
1	Bay Leaf	500g	Caster Sugar

Method

1. Heat in a pan and allow all the spices to infuse, serve warm.

Shakespeare captures the spirit of this formidable season most vividly in his beautiful 'Winter Song,' a tune that appears in his comedy, *Love's Labour's Lost*:

When icicles hang by the wall,
And Dick, the Shepherd blows his nail,
And Tim bears logs into the hall,
And milk comes frozen home in pail;

When blood is nipped, and ways be foul,
Then nightly sings the staring owl,
To-whoo;
Tu-whit, to-whoo, a merry note,
While greasy Joan doth keel the pot.

When all aloud the wind doth blow,
And coughing, drowns the parson's saw,
And birds sit brooding in the snow,
A' Marian's nose looks red and raw.

When roasted crabs hiss in the bowl,
Then nightly sings the staring owl,
To-whoo;
Tu-whit, to-whoo, a merry note,
While greasy Joan doth keel the pot.

Shakespeare's song calls to mind the frosty, bitter chill outside, but also reminds us of the wonderful, steamy warmth of the hearth within. This festive season of food, family and fun is at the heart of Shakespeare's delightful comedy *Twelfth Night, or What You Will*. As the title suggests, this play was written to be a "Twelfth Night" entertainment. The earliest recorded performance of the play was at the Inns of Court, on Candlemas Night, 2 February 1602.

"Twelfth Night," or "Epiphany Eve," which falls on the fifth of January, is the last day of Christmas festivities, and in Shakespeare's time this special day was observed with much gaiety and merry-making. Food and drink were of course at the centre of "Twelfth Night" celebrations.

Shakespeare's play mirrors the merriment, hi-jinks, and pranks that were prominent features of "Twelfth Night" traditions. The play is set in the fictional locale of "Illyria", a name Shakespeare undoubtedly derived from the Latin word "illusio," which means "the act of mocking," and indeed there is much mockery in Illyria. Illyria is a world turned upside down, where nothing is quite what it seems.

The shipwrecked heroine, Viola, lands on Illyria's coast. She disguises herself as a boy, renames herself Cesario, and enters the service of Orsino, the Duke of Illyria. Orsino is love with Olivia, a neighbouring countess, and he sends Viola (Cesario) to woo Olivia on his behalf. Mayhem ensues as the disguised Viola falls in love with Orsino, and the Countess Olivia falls in love with 'Cesario'. To add to the confusion, Viola's (Cesario's) identical twin brother, Sebastian, arrives, having landed in the same locale as his sister.

Merriment and festive misrule thrive in Countess Olivia's household. Her uncle, Sir Toby Belch, presides over nightly, drunken revels, much to the annoyance of Olivia's prim and straitlaced steward, Malvolio. When Malvolio puts an end to the carousing, Sir Toby and his fellows take swift, cruel, comic revenge. In the end, order is restored and the chaotic world is again set aright. Viola's true identity is revealed, and Orsino takes her for his wife. There is also nuptial joy for Olivia and Sebastian.

The couplings at the end of the play resemble a key feature of Elizabethan "Twelfth Night" celebrations ⸗ the selection of a "King" and "Queen" to rule (or misrule) the evening's festivities. Selection of the Twelfth Night King and Queen was made by means of the **"Twelfth Cake"**. Within these delicious cakes were hidden a bean and a pea, or two coins, and those who received the slices containing them were designated as king and queen of the night's revels.

The poet, Robert Herrick captured merry spirit of the Elizabethan winter table in his poem,

"Twelfe-Night, or King and Queene":

> Now, now the mirth comes
> With the cake full of figs and plums,
> Where beane's the king of the sport here
> Beside we know,
> The pea also
> Must revel, as queene in the court here.
>
> Next crowne the bowl ful,
> With gentle lambs-wooll;
> Adde sugar, nutmeg, and ginger,
> With a store of ale, too,
> To make the wassaile a swinger!

The recipes in this chapter capture and re⸗create the joyous, festive spirit of this season, too.

Winter Celebrations

Winter, the coldest of seasons, short days, snow, ice, wind and rain all tend to make the season gloomy, but winter sun is bright, if not too warm, and the air is crisp and can fill you with vigour. We tend to eat filling hot dishes such as stews, hearty soups and pies to ward off the cold.

People change their moods and habits in the gloom of winter which have given rise to "seasonal affective disorder" in people who get particularly depressed at this time. In Greek mythology Hades kidnapped Persephone from Demeter, the Earth goddess, because he wanted her for his wife. Zeus ordered Hades to return her but, because he tricked her into eating the food of the dead, Zeus decided that she should spend half the year with Hades and the other half with Demeter. Because of this Demeter was sad and caused Winter to fall over the earth when Persephone was in the underworld. There is a similar story in Welsh folk lore about a kidnapped maiden and her lover fighting for her return - the fight is between Winter and Summer.

The gardens are virtually bare and in the 16th century the people tended to live off the food which had been preserved during the seasons leading up to Winter. Pickled dishes such as herring and some fruits, as well as dried foods, were all consumed at this time.

Festivals, such as Christmas, were a time for great celebration and the preserved foods were prepared for the Christmas feast. Dried fruits were used to make such things as fig pudding and chutneys. Other foods associated with the season are goose, poultry and boar.

Other festivals of Winter include the following:

Celtic Festivals: Samhain - 1st November, the first day of Winter and the Celtic New Year.
Winter Solstice - 21st December, Mid-Winter.
Imbolc - 1st February, their 1st day of Spring.

Christian Festivals:

Advent - four weeks leading to Christmas.
St. Nicholas Day - 6th December.
Christmas Day - 25th December.
St. Stephen's Day - 26th December.
12th Night - Epiphany Eve.
Epiphany, the arrival of the Magi - 6th January.
St. Valentine's Day - 14th February.

The dishes chosen for the winter section have all been influenced by the availability of foods during this bleak period of the year and are typical of dishes prepared in the 16th Century.

TheFOOD of LOVE

The Taste of Shakespeare in Four Seasons

Winter Season Index

Christmas Celebration

A Chestnut Soup

Take half a hundred of chestnuts, pick them, put them in an earthen pan and set them in the oven half an hour or roast them gently over a slow fire, but take care they do not burn, then peel them and set them to stew in a quart of good beef, veal or mutton broth, till they are quite tender; In the mean time , take a piece or a slice of ham or bacon, a pound of veal a pigeon beat to pieces, a bundle of sweet herbs, an onion a little pepper and mace a piece of carrot; lay the bacon at the bottom of a stew pan lay the meat and ingredients at top; set it over a slow fire till it begins to stick to the pan then put in a crust of bread, and pour in two quarts of broth; let it boil softly till one third is wasted, then strain it off and add it to the chestnuts; season it with salt and let it boil til it is well tasted, stew two pigeons in it and fry a French roll crisp; lay it in the middle of a dish, and the pigeons on each side; pour in the soup, and send it away hot.

Coney Broth

Ingredients

1	Leg of Rabbit		60g	Onion - finely chopped
60g	Carrot - ¼ cm diced		40g	Swede - ¼ cm diced
40g	Leek - sliced		40g	Fennel - sliced
60g	Washed Pearl Barley		5g	Parsley - chopped
1ltr	Water or Chicken Stock			

Method

1. Place the leg of rabbit in a pan and cover with the water, bring to boil and skim off any scum.
2. Add the vegetables and the barley and bring to the boil. Season to taste and cook for 1 hour.
3. Remove the rabbit and cut the meat from the bone. Dice the meat into ¼ cm pieces. Place back into the broth and add the chopped parsley.
4. The soup may be finished with a tablespoon of cream.

Chestnut Soup and Bacon

Ingredients

400g	Cooked Skinned Chestnuts (reserve 20g for garnish)		
100g	Smoked Bacon Pieces (reserve 20g for garnish)		
100g	Onion - sliced	**200g**	Potatoes - diced
30g	Butter	**1ltr**	Chicken Stock
5g	Ground Mace	**5g**	Mint - chopped

Method

1. Fry the bacon in the butter. Add the onion and chestnuts and cook for a few minutes without colouring.
2. Add the stock and bring to the boil, add the mace and potatoes.
3. Re-boil and check the seasoning and add the mint. Cook for 1 hour until the stock is reduced by about 1/3.
4. Fry the reserved bacon until crisp and chop it quite small. Chop the reserved chestnuts and mix with the bacon.
5. Blend the soup in a food processor and pass through a fine conical strainer. Return the soup to the pan and re-boil. Check the seasoning.
6. Pour into the serving dish and sprinkle the bacon and chestnut garnish into the soup.

Potted Lobster

Take a live lobster and boil it in salt and water, and peg it so that no water gets in; when it is cold, pick out all the flesh and body, take out the gut, beat it fine in a mortar, and season it with beaten mace, grated nutmeg, pepper and salt; mix all together; melt a piece of butter as big as a large walnut, and mix it with the lobster as you are beating it; when it is beat to a paste, put it into your potting pot, and put it down as close and hard as you can; then set some fresh butter in a deep broad pan before the fire, and when it is all melted, take off the scum at the top (if any) and pour the clear butter over the meat as thick as a crown piece; the whey and churn-milk will settle at the bottom of the pan, but take care none of that goes in, and always let your butter be very good, or you will spoil all; or only put the meat whole, with the body mixed among it, laying them as close together as you can, and pour the butter over them. You must be sure to let the lobster be well boiled. A middling one will take half an hour of boiling.

Fish Soup with Saffron

Ingredients

5oog	Fish (Haddock, Pollock, Whiting, Salmon) ⁄ all bones and skin removed and cut into thin strips

40g	Carrot	40g	Celery
40g	Fennel	40g	Onion ⁄ thinly sliced
2	Cloves of Crushed Garlic	20g	Tomato Paste
40g	Tomatoes ⁄ seeds removed and neatly chopped		
5g	Saffron Strands	10g	Chopped Parsley
5g	Thyme ⁄ rubbed	1fl oz	Olive Oil
1.5 ltr	Fish Stock	Juice	of 1 lemon

Method

1. Cut the fish into ½ cm pieces and fry quickly in the olive oil.
2. Add the vegetables, but not the tomato, and fry for 2 – 3 minutes without colouring.
3. Add the tomato paste and mix in well. Add the lemon juice and the stock. Bring to the boil and then simmer. Add the saffron and thyme, season to taste.
4. Cook for 1 hour and add the tomato pieces and the parsley.
   Serve with toasted sippets of rustic bread.

Fried Oysters with Chilli Sauce

Ingredients

24	Oysters - removed from shell and dried on kitchen paper		
5g	Ground Mace	5g	Ground Nutmeg
4	Whites of Egg - beat lightly to break up the gel.		
100g	Cornflour	Oil - to fry	

Method

1. Mix the cornflour. the mace and nutmeg together.
2. Heat the oil in a pan or heat your deep fat fryer to 180°C.
3. Pass the oysters through the cornflour then the egg white. Re-pass the oysters through the cornflour.
4. Fry the oysters until crisp and golden in colour, drain on kitchen paper.
5. Serve with the chilli sauce, garnish with fresh herbs and lemon.

For the sauce

30g	Red Chilli - chopped fine	60g	Onion - chopped fine
30g	Butter	90g	Sugar
100g	Tomatoes - chopped	2fl oz	Wine Vinegar
60g	Honey	200ml	Chicken Stock

Method

1. Cook the onion and chilli in the butter until soft, add the wine vinegar, sugar and honey and bring to the boil.
2. Add stock and the tomatoes.
3. Cook for 30 minutes and then blend in a food processor, check seasoning and serve with the oysters.

Broiled Whiting with Prawns in Butter Sauce

Ingredients

500g	Whiting – filleted and skinned	100g	Cooked Prawns
1	Lemon	30g	Shallot – finely chopped
60g	Flour	5g	Ground Nutmeg
90g	Butter	2fl oz	Oil

Method

1. Dry the fish on kitchen paper.
2. Mix the flour and the nutmeg together and add a pinch of salt.
3. Preheat your grill. Pass the fish through the flour and place it skinned side down onto a greased baking tray. Brush the fish with oil and set under the grill.
4. Cook on each side until golden – about 4 minutes each side.
5. Melt 1/3 of the butter in a pan and cook the shallot without colouring. Add the prawns and cook for 2 minutes. Add the lemon juice and reduce by half, remove from heat. Stir in the rest of the butter and check the seasoning.
6. Dress the whiting on a plate and pour the sauce over and around the fish. Garnish with fresh herbs.

Potted Crayfish

Ingredients

30g	Butter		2fl oz	White Wine
150ml	Double Cream		30g	Shallot - finely diced
5g	Red Chilli - finely diced		5g	Chopped Parsley and Chervil
120g	Cooked Crayfish Tails			

Method

1. Sweat the shallot in the butter and add the chilli. Add the crayfish.
2. Add the wine and reduce by 2/3.
3. Add the cream and bring to boil, check the seasoning and reduce until very thick. Stir in the herbs and place in ramekins and chill.

These may be served hot or cold. If served hot leave in ramekin. If you want them cold, warm the ramekin in hot water and turn out onto a plate.

To make fine Sausages

You must take six pounds of good pork free from skin, gristle and fat, cut it very small and beat it in a mortar till it is very fine, then shred six pounds of beef suet very fine and free from all skin, shred it as fine as possible; take a good deal of sage wash it very clean, pick off the leaves and shred it very fine; spread your meat on a clean dresser or table, then shake the sage all over, about three large spoonfuls; shred the thin rind of a middling lemon very fine and throw over, with as many sweet herbs (when shred fine) as will fill a large spoon; grate two nutmegs over, throw over two spoonfuls of pepper a large spoonful of salt, then throw over the suet and mix it all well together; put it down close in a pot; when you use them roll them up with as much egg as will make them roll smooth; make them the size of a sausage and fry them in butter or good dripping; be sure it be hot before you put them in, and keep rolling them about: when they are thorough hot and of a fine light brown, they are enough.

Gobbets of Pork in a Sharp Sauce

Ingredients

600g	Pork Shoulder - diced	60g	Flour
60g	Butter	150g	Onion - diced
5g	English Mustard	150g	Apple - peeled & cut ¼ cm diced
90g	Gherkin - cut into fine strips	100g	Sultanas
250ml	Cider	100ml	Cider Vinegar
90g	Sugar	5g	Parsley - chopped
5g	Sage - chopped	1/2ltr	Chicken Stock

Method

1. Mix the pork with the flour and shake off the excess.
2. Fry the pork in the butter and then add the onion. Cook for 5 minutes until browned.
3. Add the tomato and mix in well. Add the stock and cider and cider vinegar gradually. Add the mustard.
4. Bring to the boil and check the seasoning.
5. Add the sultanas, the apple and the sugar and cook for 1½ hours.
   If you wish to have a smooth sauce then:-
6. Strain the sauce into a food processor and place the meat back into the pan. Process the sauce and strain it back over the meat. Bring to the boil and check the seasoning.
7. Garnish the pork with strips of gherkin and the chopped herbs.

Collops of Beef in Ale with Walnuts

Ingredients

500g	Rump Steak - cut into thin slices	200g	Onion - finely diced
3	Cloves Garlic - crushed	200g	Walnut Halves - blanched
30g	Flour		Butter - for frying
60g	Tomato Paste	60g	Sugar
250ml	Brown Ale	250ml	Beef Stock

Method

1. Coat the beef in the flour and then shake off the excess.
2. Fry the beef in the butter until browned and then add the onion and garlic, cook for 3 minutes.
3. Add the tomato paste and mix in well. Add the sugar and the ale and bring to the boil. Add the stock and check the seasoning. Add the walnuts and cook for 2 hours, simmering.
4. When the liquid has reduced by 2/3 check the seasoning and serve.

Roast Partridge with Red Cabbage and Bread Sauce

Ingredients

2	Dressed Partridges		4	Rashers Streaky Bacon
1	Large Onion - cut in half			
2	Large Carrots - peeled and cut in half length ways			
60g	Goose Fat		20g	Butter

Method

1. Remove the wishbone from the partridge, cover the breast with the bacon and secure it with string.
2. Roast the partridge on top of the onion and carrot in the goose fat in a hot, preheated oven, for 20 minutes - basting frequently.
3. When cooked allow to rest in a warm place for 15 – 20 minutes.
4. Remove the bacon from the breast and reserve. Cut the legs from the bird and keep warm.
5. Remove the breasts from the bird and keep warm.
6. Drain off the excess fat from the roasting tray and heat on top of the stove. When hot, pour in the stock and stir in the sediment from the tray and check the seasoning. Reduce by half and pass through a fine strainer or some muslin cloth into a sauce boat.
7. Keep sauce warm with the partridge.
8. To serve, place some drained red cabbage on the centre of the plate, put the breast of partridge on top of the cabbage. Cut the bacon into strips and place on the breast. Cut the leg into drumstick and thigh and serve to the side of the breast.
9. Pour some roast gravy around the dish and serve bread sauce apart, garnish with watercress.

Roast Gravy
Ingredients

5oo ml	Good Chicken Stock

Bread Sauce
Ingredients

40g	White Breadcrumbs		1	Onion - studded with cloves
1	Bay leaf		10 fl oz	Milk
15g	Butter		Pinch	Ground Nutmeg
6	Cloves			

Method

1. Boil the milk, infusing it with the onion studded with cloves and bay leaf for 15 minutes - then remove from the milk.
2. Stir in the breadcrumbs and simmer for 2 – 3 minutes.
3. Stir in the butter and the nutmeg. Check seasoning and serve.

continued..........

.....continued

Red Cabbage

Ingredients

500g	Red Cabbage - sliced	150g	Sliced Apple - peeled and cored
60g	Sugar	150ml	Red Wine
50ml	Red Wine Vinegar		

Method

1. Place all the ingredients in a thick bottomed pan and heat on top of stove. Season.
2. When boiling, place the pan - with a tight fitting lid, into a moderate oven and cook for 2 hours.

Vegetables Available in the Winter Season

Recipe suggestions for Vegetables can be found in the chapter on Salads and Vegetables.

Carrots, Parsnips, Turnips, Beetroot, Salisfy, Potatoes, Onions, Cabbage, Sprouts, Spinach, Lettuce, Endive, Jerusalem Artichokes, Leeks, Garlic, Shallots, Broccoli, Celery, Fennel.

Orange Cakes

Take the peels of four oranges, being fresh pared, and the meat taken out, boil them tender, and beat them small in a marble mortar; then take the meat of them, and two more oranges, your seeds and skins being picked out, and mix it with the peelings that are beaten; set them on the fire with a spoonful or two of orange flower water, keeping it stirring till that moisture be pretty well dried up; then have ready to every pound of pulp, four pounds and a quarter of double refined sugar, make your sugar very hot, and dry it upon the fire, then mix it and the pulp together, and set it on the fire again till the sugar be very melted, but be sure it does not boil: you may put in a little peel, small, shred, or grated, and when it is cold draw it up in double papers; dry them before the fire, and when you turn them, put two together; or you may keep them in deep pots and dry them as you have occasion.

Spiced Orange Cakes with Glazed Oranges

Ingredients

80g	Flour	75g	Salt Free Butter ⁄ melted
80g	Caster Sugar	30g	Ground Almonds
Pinch	Cinnamon	2	Oranges ⁄ zest only, flesh reserved
3	Eggs		

Method

1. Whisk the eggs and sugar to ribbon stage ⁄ it should be very pale and hold the marks of the whisk in the mixture.
2. Fold the flour, almonds, cinnamon and orange zest gently into the egg mixture.
3. Gradually fold the butter into the mixture, being careful not to get any of the white solids in with the cake mix.
4. Pour the mix into greased and floured small cake or tartlet moulds. Rest the mix for at least 1 hour.
5. Bake in a preheated oven 190°C for 8 – 9 minutes until firm to the touch. Rest in the moulds until cooled and turn out, dust with icing sugar.

Oranges

Ingredients

2　Oranges ⁄ cut into rounds
120g　Caster Sugar
60g　Butter

Method

1. Remove the pith from the orange with a sharp knife and cut the orange across into rounds ½ cm thick, drain.
2. Melt butter in a frying pan and add the oranges. Turn when coloured, add sugar and allow to caramelize.
3. Remove from heat and cool.

Serve the orange cakes and the caramelized oranges with the syrup, garnish with mint.

Almond Custard

Ingredients

475ml	Double Cream	100g	Ground Almonds
6	Eggs	100g	Caster Sugar
Pinch	Ground Nutmeg		

Method

1. Warm the cream, almonds and sugar - do not boil.
2. Remove cream from the heat and whisk in the eggs and nutmeg.
3. Pour into ramekins and place in a baking tray ½ full of hot water.
   Bake in a pre-heated oven at 160°C for 45 minutes.
4. These may be served hot or cold, accompanied by poached fruit such as pears or apples.

Apple and Lemon Tart in a Cinnamon Cream

Ingredients

500g	Apples - peeled cored and diced	120g	Caster Sugar
350ml	Double Cream	80g	Salt Free Butter
5g	Cinnamon	Pinch	Nutmeg
3	Lemons - juice and grated zest only		
300g	Sweet Pastry	5	Eggs

Method

1. Grease a large 10 inch flan tin.
2. Line the flan with the sweet pastry making sure you prick the bottom with a fork. Bake blind.
3. Cook the apples in the butter and add the sugar and the cinnamon. Cool when the apples begin to lose their shape. Add the lemon juice and the zest.
4. Mix the eggs and the cream together and combine with the apples. Fill the flan case with the mixture.
5. Bake in a moderate oven 180°C for 45 minutes.
6. When cold dust with icing sugar and nutmeg.

This dish could be accompanied by a compote of blackberries.

To Make Poore Knights

Cut two penny loaves in round slices, dip them in half a pint of cream or faire water, then lay them abroad in a dish, and beat three eggs and grated nutmegs and sugar, beat them with the cream then melt some butter in a frying pan, and wet the sides of the toasts and lay them in on the wet side, then pour in the rest upon them, serve in with rosewater, sugar and butter.

Lobster Soup

Ingredients

500g	Cooked Lobster shell ⁄ reserve flesh for garnish		
60g	Small Carrot ⁄ diced	6og	Small Fennel ⁄ diced
6og	Small Onion ⁄ diced	60g	Small Celery ⁄ diced
60g	Salt Free Butter	30g	Tomato Paste
10g	Tarragon ⁄ chopped	2 fl oz	Brandy
1ltr	Fish Stock	100ml	Double Cream

Method

1. Remove the cooked lobster from the shell and dice it into quite small pieces, reserve for the garnish. Break the shell up into small pieces.
2. Fry the shell in half of the butter in a deep pan, cook for a few minutes then add the vegetables and cook for 3 minutes.
3. Add the tomato paste and mix in thoroughly. Add the brandy and flame, add the fish stock and the tarragon then bring to the boil and season. Cook for 30 minutes.
4. Mix the remaining butter with the flour in a bowl and make into small balls. Strain the soup and remove the shell, blend the vegetables in a liquidizer.
5. Re⁄boil the soup, add the flour balls and whisk into the soup, which will thicken and will only require to be cooked for 5 minutes. Add the cream and check the seasoning.
6. Garnish with the diced lobster and a little tarragon.

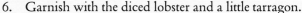

Ophelia's Salad

Ingredients

250g	Cooked Artichoke Bottoms - cut in ¼	200g	Cooked Asparagus - tips only
150g	Celeriac - cut into fine strips and marinaded in lemon juice		
150g	Sauteed Oyster Mushrooms	150g	Cooked Small Potatoes - cut in slices
200g	Mixed Lettuce Leaves	4	Red Roses

Dressing

4 parts	Olive Oil	1 part	Cider Vinegar
1 tspn	Sugar	Taste	Salt
Taste	Ground Pepper	1 tspn	Tewkesbury Mustard

Method - Mix all together and whisk until an emulsion forms

Method

1. Wash the leaves in cold water, shake off all excess water. Tear the leaves and place in a bowl.
2. Mix the artichokes, potatoes and mushrooms in some of the dressing.
3. Separate the rose petals from the stalk and wash them, dry very gently on kitchen paper.
4. Arrange lettuce leaves in the centre of a plate in a slight dome, place some of the artichoke mixture on top and garnish with the asparagus and rose petals.
5. Serve extra dressing with the salad.

Ballotine of Duck with Chicken and Pistachio Nuts and Wild Boar Sausages

Ingredients

1	2kg Duck	1	1.5kg Chicken
200g	Minced Pork	3	Eggs
200ml	Double Cream	2g	Ground Nutmeg
200g	Pistachio Nuts - peeled. (Boil for 5 minutes, drain and then rub in a kitchen towel to remove the skin.)		Seasoning

Method

To bone out the duck.

1. Lay the duck on its breast and make a cut from the neck to the parson's nose with a small sharp knife.
2. Tease the knife along the back bone on each side gently pushing the flesh from the bones, being careful not to cut through the skin.
3. Move your knife around the wing joint and dislocate the joint. Tease the flesh away moving down to the breast bone, being careful as the flesh is very thin over the breast bone. Gently pull the flesh away and again tease it with the knife. Repeat this on the other side and pull the carcase away.
4. Scrape the flesh away from the legs of the bird from the inside and pull the bones out.
5. The winglets can be cut off.

The filling

1. Take the pork and place it in a food processor. Blend in the eggs, season and taste.
2. Gradually add the cream and nutmeg, do not over blend. Check seasoning, fold in the pistachio nuts and keep in the fridge.
3. Remove the skin from the chicken and cut the legs off. Then cut the breast and wing off together.
4. Dice the leg meat up, leave the breasts whole.
5. Mix the leg meat in with the pistachio nuts and pork.

continued..........

.....continued

Assembling the Ballotine

1. Lay the duck out flat on top of some oiled foil skin side down, leg towards you.
2. Season the carcase, spread half of the pork mixture over the duck.
3. Place the seasoned breasts of chicken down the centre of the duck and cover with the rest of the pork mixture.
4. Roll up the duck to form a big sausage. Roll several times in the foil and twist the ends to seal the parcel.
5. Roast the duck in a moderate oven for 2 hour. The best way to guage the cooking time is to use a temperature probe and probe to 70°C. Then allow to rest for 40 minutes.
6. The duck may be served hot or col.
7. Slice as required and serve.

Wild Boar Sausages

Ingredients

250g	Wild Boar Mince	100g	Breadcrumbs
20cl	Water	3g	Ground Ginger
3g	Ground Mace	3g	Ground Nutmeg
3g	Chopped Sage	60g	GratedApple
½ Tspn	Ground Black Pepper	½ Tspn	Ground White Pepper
1	Bunch Natural Sausage Skins (wash before use in cold running water)		

Method

1. Mix all the ingredients together and taste.
2. Either by using a piping bag or a machine, fill the sausage skins to your required size sausage. Twist the ends to seal each sausage.
3. When all sausages are finished, place in the fridge to firm up.
4. If you wish you can blanch the sausages in boiling water for 4 minutes before frying which will stop them bursting. Make sure you dry them on kitchen paper before frying.
5. They can also be wrapped in bacon and baked in the oven.

Serves 6 - 8 people

Fig Pudding with Apple Snow

Ingredients
Suet Pastry

225g	Flour	100g	Suet
15g	Baking Powder	2½ fl oz	Water
Pinch	Salt		

150 ml	Brandy	250g	Dried Figs ⁄ chopped
100g	Raisins	50g	Dried Apricots ⁄ chopped
50g	Grated Apple	5g	Ginger
5g	Cinnamon	25g	Honey

Method
1. Rub the suet into the flour, salt and baking powder.
2. Add the water and mix to a dough, rest in cool place.
3. Mix all other ingredients and allow to marinade for 1 hour.
4. Line a large greased pudding basin with 2/3 of the suet pastry.
5. Place the fruit mix into the pastry lined basin and moisten the top edge of the pastry.
6. Cover the fruit with the remaining paste and crimp the edges together.
7. Cover the pudding with some greaseproof paper or greased foil and secure around the top of the pudding. Steam in a large saucepan, half full of hot water, for 2 hours.
8. Turn out when cooked. Serve with some apple snow.

continued..........

.....continued

Apple Snow

Ingredients

500g	Apples - diced	90g	Sugar
Pinch	Ground Cinnamon	60g	Salt Free Butter
Pinch	Ground Ginger		
3	Egg Whites	150g	Sugar
4 drops	Vanilla Extract	1tspn	Lemon Juice
10 fl oz	Double Cream	60g	Sugar

Method

1. Melt the butter and cook the apples and sugar, together with the cinnamon and ginger, until they fall to a puree. Allow to cool.
2. Whisk the egg whites and sugar with the lemon juice and vanilla to form a peak, this is best achieved with an electric whisk.
3. Whisk the cream, sugar and vanilla to a piping consistency.
4. Fold the apple mixture through the cream, then fold the meringue mix through the cream and chill.
5. Serve with the fig pudding garnished with crystallized violets.

VEGETABLES

There's fennel for you and columbines: there's rue for you; and here's some for me: may we call it herb Grace o' Sundays: O you must wear your rue with a difference.

Ophelia
Hamlet Prince of Denmark

Vegetables have always been an important part of our diet, both from an economic and a nutritional standpoint. Therefore the purchasing of sound fresh vegetables is vital to the nutritional balance of a meal.

Choosing Vegetables

Root Vegetables
Carrots, swede, turnips, must be firm, free of any soil and without any score marks from spades. They should be of an even size and with no blemishes to the skin.

Leaf and Flower Vegetables
Such as cabbage and brussels sprouts, should be crisp, fresh and have bright coloured leaves. They should be tight and compact and free from soil and sand. Cauliflower and broccolis should be firm and compact, with no sign of seeding.

Stems
Stems such as salsify and celery should also be firm, white and clean.

Tubers
Tubers such as potatoes and Jerusalem artichokes should be firm and free from spade marks and soil.

Fruits
Fruits such as tomatoes, peppers and cucumbers should be firm with a good colour and without blemish or damage to the outer skin.

Bulbs
Bulbs such as onions, leeks, garlic and shallots should again be firm and clean.

Pods
Pods such as peas and beans should be crisp, with a good colour and not too big.

Fungi
Mushrooms such as: Cepes, Chanterelles, Morels, Cup, Flat, Oyster and Shitake must be free of dirt and grit, and should be quite firm.

To Make Beans Ragooed with Cabbage

Take a nice little cabbage, about the size of a pint bason; when the outside leaves, top and stalks are cut off, half boil it, cut a hole in the middle pretty big, take what you cut out and chop it very fine, with a few of the beans boiled, a carrot boiled and mashed, and a turnip boiled, mash all together, put them into a sauce pan, season them with pepper, salt, and nutmeg, a good piece of butter, stew them a few minutes over the fire, stirring the pan often; in the meantime put the cabbage into a sauce pan, but take great care it does not fall to pieces; put to it four spoonfuls of water, two of wine, and one of mushroom pickle, a piece of butter rolled in a little flour, a very little pepper; cover it close, let it stew softly till it is tender; then take it up carefully and lay it in the middle of a dish pour in your mashed roots in the middle and fill it up high and your ragoo round it.

Braised Cabbage Parcels

Ingredients

1	500g Cabbage	150g	Carrot ⁄ cooked and mashed
150g	Swede ⁄ cooked and mashed	30g	Butter
Pinch	Caraway Seed	Pinch	Nutmeg
300ml	Vegetable Stock	1 Tspn	Cornflour

Mirepoix for base of braising liquor

100g	Chopped Leek	100g	Chopped Onion
50g	Chopped Celery	100g	Chopped Carrot

Method

1. Cut the cabbage in half and separate the leaves and wash well. Blanch in boiling salted water for 4 minutes.
2. Chop the smaller leaves small. Sweat them in half of the butter and mix with the mashed carrot and swede. Season and mix in the caraway seeds.
3. Roll the cabbage and carrot, mix into balls and wrap in the blanched leaves.
4. Sweat the leek, the celery and carrot in a deep pan. Place the cabbage parcels on top of the celery etc. and pour the stock around the parcels. Season, bring to the boil and place in a hot oven for 30 minutes.
5. When cooked, remove parcels from the pan and rest. Thicken the stock in the pan with the cornflour and re⁄boil, check seasoning and pass through a fine strainer. Serve with the parcels of cabbage.

Creamed Fennel with Herbs

Ingredients

400g	Fennel - sliced	200ml	Double Cream
30g	Shallot - finely diced	30g	Salt Free Butter
5g	Chopped Chives or Fennel Herb		

Method

1. Sweat the shallot in the butter and cook for 2 – 3 minutes.
2. Add the fennel and cook for 5 minutes, add the cream and boil. Season.
3. Stir the fennel regularly to avoid catching. When cooked the cream should be reduced to a coating consistency. Add the chives and serve.

Creamed Jerusalem Artichokes

Ingredients

500g	Jerusalem Artichokes - washed, peeled & diced small		
300ml	Double Cream	Pinch	Ground Nutmeg
Sprig	Dill - chopped	1	Lemon - juice only

Method

1. Cook the artichoke in boiling, salted water with the lemon juice, do not overcook.
2. Drain the artichoke . Boil the cream in a pan and add the nutmeg. Season, reduce by 2/3 and then put in the artichokes. Reduce on a fast heat until the artichokes are well coated.
3. Sprinkle with chopped dill.

Stir Fried Artichokes with Garlic and Ginger

Ingredients

400g	Jerusalem Artichokes - peeled and sliced		
10g	Fresh Ginger - cut in fine strips		
2 cloves	Garlic - finely diced	4	Spring Onions - sliced
Sprig	Coriander - chopped	50ml	Vegetable Oil

Method

1. Quickly fry the artichokes in the oil and add the ginger. Cook for 2 – 3 minutes and add the spring onion, fry untill the onion is tender and remove all from the pan and drain. Sprinkle with chopped coriander.

Spiced Celeriac Cakes

Ingredients

400g	Celeriac - peeled and diced	400ml	Milk
50g	Flour	3	Eggs
Pinch	Nutmeg	Pinch	Ground Mace
Pinch	Paprika	Pinch	Ginger
30g	Butter	30ml	Oil

Method

1. Boil the celeriac in the milk. When cooked, drain, mash and season. Reserve the milk.
2. Mix the celeriac with the flour and eggs, add the spices, if too dry add a little of the cooking milk.
3. Fry the mix in moulds in the butter and oil until golden on each side and set.

Courgettes Filled with Goats Cheese and Chillies

Ingredients

4	Small Courgettes	100g	Goats Cheese
1	Red Chilli ⁄ finely diced with seeds removed		
30g	Salt Free Butter	30ml	Olive Oil
30g	Shallot ⁄ finely diced	25g	White Breadcrumbs
Sprig	Tarragon ⁄ chopped	Sprig	Thyme ⁄ rubbed

Method

1. Cut the ends from the courgettes and scoop the centre out with an apple corer.
2. Dice up the courgette core.
3. Sweat the shallot and chilli in the butter and add the chopped up courgette. Season and add the crumbs and crumbled up cheese, remove from heat.
4. Add the herbs and season. Put the filling into a piping bag and fill the courgette cases.
5. Place the courgettes on a greased baking sheet, brush with oil and season. Bake in a hot oven for 10 – 15 minutes.

Balsamic Glazed Shallots

Ingredients

200g	Shallots		50ml	Olive Oil
150ml	Balsamic Vinegar		25g	Brown Sugar
15g	Red Currant Jelly		350ml	Vegetable Stock

Method

1. Peel the shallots and brown in the olive oil in a shallow pan.
2. Add the vinegar, sugar and stock. Season.
3. Boil gently until shallots are cooked, then rapidly reduce the liquor to a glaze.
4. Add the red currant jelly and serve.

Baby Turnips Glazed in Cider with Prunes

Ingredients

400g	Baby Turnips ⁃ scrape clean and leave ½ cm of green top in place		
100g	Soaked Pitted Prunes ⁃ soak in white wine over night		
30ml	White Wine	200ml	Cider
50g	Honey	30g	Unsalted Butter

Method

1. Place the turnips in a shallow pan, cover with the cider ⁃ you may need to add some water to just cover the turnips.
2. Add the honey and the butter and season. Cover with a lid.
3. Boil gently until the turnips are cooked, remove the turnips and keep warm. Reduce the liquore until it is very syrupy and then toss in the turnips and prunes and serve.

Glazed Beetroot with Honey and Orange

Ingredients

500g	Beetroot ⁃ washed, cooked, topped, tailed and peeled.		
60g	Clear Honey	350ml	Orange Juice
Pinch	Ground Ginger	20g	Butter
Sprig	Chopped Mint		

Method

1. Cover the beetroot in the orange juice ⁃ you may need to add a little water, add the butter.
2. Add the honey and ginger. Boil gently until reduced to a glaze which will coate the beetroot.
3. Sprinkle with the mint.

Sautéed Asparagus with Oyster Mushrooms and Garlic

Ingredients

400g	Asparagus - peeled and trimmed	200g	Oyster Mushrooms
2	Cloves Garlic - finely diced	30ml	White Balsamic Vinegar
30g	Unsalted Butter	30ml	Olive Oil

Method

1. Pre-cook the asparagus in boiling water with plenty of salt for a minute or two, drain and dry on kitchen paper.
2. Sauté the asparagus in half of the butter and oil until lightly coloured, remove from pan and keep warm.
3. Add the rest of the butter and oil and fry the garlic. Then add the mushrooms, season well and cook for 5 – 8 minutes.
4. Add the balsamic vinegar and reduce by ½.
5. Arrange the mushrooms on a plate with the asparagus on top and drizzle with the balsamic reduction.

Broad Beans with Smoked Bacon and Caraway Seeds

Ingredients

400g	Broad Beans	**100g**	Smoked Bacon - cut in ¼ cm dice
30g	Salt Free Butter	**30g**	Shallot - finely diced

Method

1. Shell the beans and cook in boiling, salted water, do not over cook.
2. Remove the skin from the beans.
3. Fry the bacon in the butter and add the shallot, do not colour.
4. Add the beans and mix well, season, add the caraway seeds and serve.

New Potatoes with Pesto

Ingredients

400g	New Potatoes	60g	Pesto
60ml	Olive Oil	30g	Butter
10g	Chopped Purple Basil		

Method

1. Wash the potatoes and cook in boiling salted water, do not over cook, drain.
2. Melt the butter in the oil in a roasting tray, add the potatoes and put into a hot oven.
3. When lightly covered add the pesto and mix well.
4. Sprinkle with basil and serve.

Gratin Potatoes with Rosemary

Ingredients

500g	Potatoes	250ml	Single Cream
30g	Rosemary - picked and chopped	2	Cloves Garlic - crushed
60g	Grated Cheese – Cheddar or Gruyere		
Pinch	Ground Nutmeg		Seasoning

Method

1. Slice the potatoes ½ cm thick, do not wash.
2. Lay potatoes on kitchen paper, season with salt and pepper and sprinkle with rosemary.
3. Arrange the potatoes in a greased oven proof dish. Mix the garlic with the cream and bring to boil and pour over the potatoes.
4. Sprinkle the cheese over the top of the potatoes.
5. Bake in a moderate oven - 190°C, until cooked and golden brown.

Potatoes Glazed in Cider with Oregano

Ingredients

4	Large Potatoes ╱ peeled and cut into cubes 3 cm x 3cm x 1½ cm thick
60g	Salt Free Butter	**400ml** Cider
5g	Oregano

Method

1. In a non╱stick frying pan, fry the potatoes in the butter until golden brown on both sides.
2. Add the cider and cook gently until the potatoes are tender.
3. Reduce the cider to a glaze, coat the potatoes and sprinkle with the oregano.

Savoury Potatoes with Garlic and Shallots

Ingredients

400g	Potatoes - peeled and sliced into ½ cm slices		
100g	Shallots - halved and sliced thinly		
30ml	Oil	2	Cloves Garlic - finely chopped
60g	Salt Free Butter - melted	500ml	White Stock

Method

1. Fry the shallot and garlic in the oil until golden.
2. Mix the shallot with the sliced potatoes and season, place in a greased oven proof dish.
3. Arrange sliced potatoes on top neatly. Cover with the stock
4. Brush the top layer of the potatoes liberally with melted butter.
5. Bake in a hot oven, reduce the heat after half an hour and cook until all the stock has been absorbed by the potatoes and they are golden brown.

Potato Cakes with Shallot and Chives

Ingredients

400g	Potatoes	**60g**	Sliced Shallots
5g	Chopped Chives	**60g**	Salt Free Butter
	Seasoning		

Method

1. Part cook the potatoes in boiling water for 5 minutes, drain and cool.
2. Grate the potato through the largest part of the grater on to a tray, season.
3. Finely slice the shallots and chop the chives.
4. Mix the shallot and the chives with the potato.
5. Melt the butter in a non-stick frying pan and either make one big cake, or individual portions of the potato, and fry on both sides until golden brown.

Creamed Potatoes with Saffron and Chives

Ingredients

500g	Potatoes (Maris Piper)	**50g**	Butter
60ml	Cream	**Pinch**	Saffron
Pinch	Chopped Chives		

Method

1. Boil the potatoes in boiling salted water, do not overcook.
2. Drain and dry the potatoes in a warm oven.
3. Pass the potatoes through a ricer or mouli.
4. Season with salt and pepper and add the butter.
5. Heat the cream on the stove and infuse with the saffron then add to the potatoes.
6. Sprinkle with chives.

Crushed New Potato Cakes with Sweet Red Onion

Ingredients

400g	New Potatoes - cooked	100g	Sliced Red Onion
20g	Brown Sugar	50ml	Balsamic Vinegar
60g	Butter		

Method

1. Mash the potatoes in a bowl and season.
2. Sweat the onion in half of the butter and add the sugar and balsamic vinegar, reduce to a thick syrup. Cool.
3. Mix the onion with the potato and shape into potato cakes. Pass through seasoned flour and fry in the butter and oil in a non-stick frying pan.
4. When coloured on each side remove and serve.

Roast Potatoes Perfumed with Rosemary

Ingredients

500g	Potatoes ⁄ washed and peeled and re⁄washed
100g	Goose Fat
1 sprig	Rosemary ⁄ rubbed to remove the stem

Method

1. Boil the potatoes for 5 minutes and cool in cold water, drain.
2. Draw a fork down the length of the potato scoring the sides and fluffing them up.
3. Melt the fat in a roasting tray and put in the potatoes in, moving them about so as they are covered in the fat, season and toss in the rosemary.
4. Roast in a moderate oven until golden brown and crisp.
5. When cooked (test by pushing a small knife into the potato) drain before serving.

A Dish of Leeks with Pork and Almonds

To make white leeks, he who is in charge of them should arrange that he has his leeks and slice them small and wash them very well and put to boil, and take a good piece of chine of pork and clean it very well and put it to boil herewith; and when they are well boiled take them out on to fair and clean tables, and let them save the broth in which they were boiled, and let there be a good mortar full of blanched almonds, and ten take the broth in which the said leeks have boiled and draw up the almonds with it, and if there is not enough of said broth take beef or mutton broth and take care that it is not too salty; and then afterward put our bruet to boil in a fair and clean pot, and then chop your leeks and bray them in a mortar; and being brayed, put them into your broth of almonds as much as water, to boil and the leeks being boiled when it comes to the side board put your meat on a serving dish and pout the broth and leeks over.

Sir Toby's Leek and Bacon Bruet

Ingredients

500g	Smoked Streaky Bacon	500g	Leeks ⁄ sliced & washed
200g	Sliced Onion	200g	Ground Almonds
50g	Butter	25g	Grated Fresh Ginger
400ml	White Stock	100ml	Double Cream
100ml	White Wine	½ tspn	Cornflour

Method

1. Fry the bacon in the butter and add the onion, leek and ginger, cook for 8 – 10 minutes. Season.
2. Add the wine and reduce by ½ . Add the almonds, then add the stock and reduce by ½ .
3. Add cream re-boil and reduce by ½ .
4. Thicken with the cornflour if required.
5. Seve in a soup plate with creamed potatoes.

SALADS

To Make a Sallad of Limons

Take the rinds of Limons cut in halves, and boil them in several waters till they are very tender, then take Vinegar, Water and Sugar, and make a Syrup, then put in your Limons, first cut as you would an Apple-paring, round and round till you come at the top, boil them a while in the Syrup, then set them by till the next day, then boil them again a little, and so do till you see they be clear, and the Syrup thick; when you serve them to the Table, wash them in Vinegar.

To Make a Grand Sallad

Take a fair broad brimm'd dish, and in the middle of it lay some pickled Limon Pill, then lay round about it each sort by themselves, Olives, Capers, Broom Buds, Ash Keys, Purslane pickled, and French Beans pickled, and little Cucumbers pickled, and Barberries pickled, and Clove Gilliflowers, Cowslips, Currans, Figs, blanched Almonds and Raisins, Slices of Limon with Sugar on them, Dates stoned and sliced. Garnish your Dish brims with Candied Orange, Limon and Citron Pill, and some Candied Eringo roots.

To Make a Sallad with Fresh Salmon

Your Salmon being boiled and souced, mince some of it small with Apples and Onyons, put thereto Oyl, Vinegar, and Pepper; so serve it to the Table: Garnish your Dish with Limon and Capers.

To Make Boiled Sallads

Boil some Carots very tender, and scrape them to pieces like the Pulp of an Apple, season them with Cinamon and Ginger and Sugar, put in Currans, a little Vinegar, and a piece of sweet Butter, stew these in a Dish, and when they begin to dry put in more Butter and a little Salt, so serve them to the Table, thus you may do Lettuce, or Spinage or Beets.

To Make a Sorrel Sallad

Take a quantity of Sorrel picked clean and washed, boil it with water and a little Salt, and when it is enough, drain it and butter it, and put in a little Vinegar and Sugar into it, then garnish it with hard Eggs and Raisin.

Rosalind's Salad

Ingredients

200g	French Beans – cooked cut in ½ cm pieces		
60g	Finely Chopped Shallot		
60g	Carrot – cut in fine strips	80g	Sliced Cooked Mushrooms
1	Red Pepper – seeds removed & diced small		
50ml	Honey	½ tsp	English Mustard
100ml	Olive Oil	1	Lemon – juice only
2	Red Roses – petals only, shredded		

Method

1. Blend the honey, oil and mustard with the lemon juice and season.
2. Mix the beans and the peppers with some of the dressing and arrange in a round mould on a plate, tamp the beans down and arrange the mushrooms on top.
3. Arrange the carrot on top and dress with the rose petals.

Ophelia's Salad

Ingredients

250g	Cooked Artichoke Bottoms - cut in ¼	200g	Cooked Asparagus, tips only
150g	Fine strips of Celeriac - marinaded in lemon juice		
150g	Sauteed Oyster Mushrooms	150g	Cooked Small Potatoes - cut in slices
200g	Mixed Lettuce Leaves	5	Red Roses

Dressing

4 parts	Olive Oil	**1 parts**	Cider Vinegar
1 tspn	Sugar	**Taste**	Salt
Taste	Ground Pepper	**1 tspn**	Tewkesbury Mustard

Mix all together and whisk until an emulsion forms

Method

1. Wash the leaves in cold water shake off all excess water. Tear the leaves and place in a bowl.
2. Mix the artichokes, potatoes and mushrooms in some of the dressing.
3. Separate the rose petals from the stalk and wash them, dry very gently on kitchen paper.
4. Arrange lettuce leaves in the centre of a plate in a slight dome, place some of the artichoke mixture on top and garnish with the asparagus and rose petals.
5. Serve extra dressing with the salad.

Miranda's Salad

Ingredients

300g	Red Cabbage - finely shredded, and blanched.		
150g	Apples - grated	60g	Onion - finely shredded
100g	Smoked Streaky Bacon - diced and cooked crisp		
75ml	Olive Oil	25ml	Balsamic Vinegar
4	Rosemary Flowers	25ml	Lemon Juice
	Honey		

Method

1. In a deep pot heat the vinegar and the lemon juice and add the onion and the apple. Cover with a lid and boil for 5 minutes. Add the honey and then cool.
2. Arrange the salad on lettuce leaves, sprinkle with the bacon and garnish with the rosemary flowers.

Viola's Salad

Ingredients

1	Belgian Chicory	100g	Tomatoes - cut in ¼, seeds removed
4	Artichoke Bottoms - sliced	60g	Green Pepper - diced
4	Quail Eggs	Sprig	Chervil - chopped
Sprig	Tarragon - chopped	50ml	Mustard Dressing

Method

1. Slice the tomatoes, peppers and artichokes roughly the same size.
2. Marinade the vegetables in the dressing.
3. Gently poach the quail eggs, dress the vegetables on lettuce leaves.
4. Place a poached egg on top of the vegetables and sprinkle with the herbs.

Juliet's Salad

Ingredients

400g	Pears ⁄ peeled cored and cut in ½ cm dice		
100g	Asparagus Tips ⁄ cooked	**100g**	Celery ⁄ peeled and cut in fine dice
250g	Very Small New Potatoes ⁄ cooked	**2**	Bunches Watercress
10g	Borage with Flowers	**100ml**	Olive Oil
25ml	Cider Vinegar	**½ tspn**	Dijon Mustard

Method

1. Mix the oil and vinegar with the mustard and season.
2. Marinade the pears in the dressing with the celery.
3. Wash the watercress and pick the leaves from the stalks.
4. Slice the potatoes and arrange them on a plate in a tight circle.
5. Arrange the pears and celery on top of the potato.
6. Mix the watercress with a little dressing and mould on top of the pear.
7. Chop the borage leaves and sprinkle over the cress, dress with the flowers.
8. Arrange the asparagus around the potato base and dress with some of the dressing.

Cressida's Salad

Ingredients

2	Oranges - cut in segments	2	Watercress
30g	Mitsuna	100g	Beetroot - cut in fine strips
100g	Pea Shoots	60ml	Olive Oil
60ml	Double Cream	15ml	Lemon Juice
Pinch	Sugar	Pinch	Ground Ginger
4	Pansy Flower Heads		

Method

1. Mix the double cream and lemon juice and add sugar and ginger.
2. Dress the oranges with the cream.
3. Mix the cress with the mitsuna and beetroot and dress with the oil.
4. Arrange the cress on a plate, place oranges on top, garnish with the pansy heads and pea shoots.
5. Drizzle any orange juice from the segments around the salad.

Cleopatra's Salad

Ingredients

200g	Cooked Rice	100g	Red Pepper - finely diced
100g	Peas - cooked	200g	Button Mushrooms - diced and cooked
100g	Artichoke Bottoms - sliced		
150g	Smoked Streaky Bacon - cut in dice and fried crisp		
100ml	Olive Oil	30ml	White Wine Vinegar
½ tspn	French Mustard	Pinch	Sugar
2 tspn	Lemon Juice	100g	Palm Hearts - cut into slices

Method

1. Blend the oil, vinegar, mustard and seasoning together.
2. Mix the peppers, peas and artichokes with the rice and pour over the dressing.
3. Arrange the palm hearts around the rice, moisten with a little of the dressing.
4. Arrange the rice on a plate and sprinkle over the bacon.

115

Cordelia's Salad

Ingredients

200g	Apples - cut in fine strips	**150g**	Celery - peeled and cut in batons
	Blanched flaked almonds - lightly toasted		
100g	Raisins	**80ml**	Double cream
Pinch	Sugar		Salt and pepper
1	Lemon - juice only	**Sprig**	Coriander - chopped
Sprig	Mint - chopped		

Method

1. Make sure all the salad ingredients are clean and fresh.
2. Mix the apples and celery with the raisins and add the lemon juice.
3. Lightly whip the cream until it is of a coating consistency.
4. Mix with the fruit and celery.
5. Dress the mixture on lettuce leaves and sprinkle with almonds and herbs.

"Daffodils that come before the swallow dares, and take
The winds of March with beauty; violets dim,
But sweeter than the lids of Juno's eyes
Or Cytherea's breath; pale primroses,
That die unmarried, ere they behold
Bright Phoebus in his strength, a malady
Most incidents to maids; bold oxlips and
The crown imperial; lilies of all kinds"

(The Winter's Tale 1V.4)

"What's in a name? That which we call a rose
by any other name would smell so sweet"

(Romeo and Juliet)

Ophelia: "There's rosemary, that's for remembrance. Pray you, love,
Remember. And there is pansies, that's for thoughts."

Laertes: "A document is madness! Thoughts and remembrance fitted."

Ophelia: "There's fennel for you, and columbines. There's rue for you,
And here's some for me. We may call it herb of grace o' Sundays.
O, you must wear your rue with a difference! There's a daisy.
would give you some violets, but they withered all when my father died.
They say he made a good end."

(Ophelia's speech from Hamlet)

F lowers have been linked with food since ancient times. In the book written by the Roman, Apicius there are recipes for rose wine and violet wine. Rose water was used by the doctor, Nicander as far back as 140BC.

We still use flowers for flavouring in our everyday lives in such things as teas and tisanes. Liqueurs, wines and sugars are flavoured with flower extracts such as jasmine, elderflower, rose, apple blossom, sloe, lotus and carnation.

Flowers should only be gathered on a dry day after the dew has dried. Wash them and then shake dry, or they can be dried out completely for use out of season.

Candied Flower Petals

Ingredients

250g	Caster Sugar	5fl oz	Rose Water
Pinch	Cream of Tartar		Flower Petals - very dry

Method

1. Boil the mixture until it reaches 107°C, this is thread degree.
2. Using tweezers, dip the petals into the syrup and then place them on caster sugar and cover them with sugar.
3. When the petals are dry, shake off excess sugar and store in air tight containers between silicone paper.
4. Use for decorating sweets and ice cream or cakes.

Rosehip Relish

Ingredients

250g	Rosehips - pips removed	250ml	Red Wine Vinegar
250ml	Balsamic Vinegar	60g	Grated Fresh Ginger
200g	Raisins	400g	Apple - chopped & peeled
250g	Brown Sugar	1	Orange Juice & finely grated Zest
Pinch	Ground Cloves	15g	Red Chillies - finely diced
100g	Finely Chopped Onion	150g	Red Pepper - seeds removed & diced

Method

1. Bring the vinegar to the boil and add the rose hips. Cook until soft, remove the hips from the vinegar and pass through a sieve to remove the seeds.
2. Add the rest of the ingredients to the vinegar and replace the pulp of the rosehips in the mixture.
3. Simmer gently until the mixture is thick and syrupy, stirring occasionally.
4. Cool and store in sterilised Kilner jars.

This relish will improve with age.

Violet and Damson Jam

Ingredients

600g	Damsons - stones removed	250g	Sugar
1	Orange Juice & Zest - finely grated		
10	Violets - petals only, washed & dried.		
Pinch	Ground Ginger		

Method

1. Boil all the ingredients gently for 50 minutes, stirring occasionally.
2. Cool and place into kilner jars.

Primrose Flan

Ingredients

200g	Sweet Pastry	15g	Ground Almonds
600g	Apples - cored and peeled	Pinch	Cinnamon
100g	Caster Sugar	8	Primroses - petals only
5g	Icing Sugar		

Method

1. Roll the pastry out on the ground almonds and line a greased 8 inch flan ring on a greased baking sheet.
2. Dice 2/3 of the apples and cook in the butter until they start to fall to a puree. Add the sugar and cinnamon, cool.
3. Place the apple compound in the flan, sprinkle with some of the primrose petals and a little sugar.
4. Slice the remaining apples and fan them around the top of the flan over the petals. Sprinkle the remaining petals over the top layer of apple and sprinkle with sugar.
5. Bake in a moderate oven until the pastry is set and crisp.
6. Remove from oven and cool before removing flan ring.
7. Dust with icing sugar.

Nasturtium Vinegar

Ingredients

White Wine Vinegar   Nasturtium Petals

Method

1. Half fill a large jar with the petals, cover with vinegar and store in the sunlight.
2. When the flowers sink, top up with more petals.
3. Leave for as long as possible so that the vinegar can extract as much flkavour as possible from the flowers.

Chilled Cherry and Rose Soup

Ingredients

450g	Pitted Fresh Cherries	30g	Caster Sugar
175ml	Good Red Wine	1	Lemon - cut into slices
450ml	Water	1	Cinnamon Stick
Pinch	Ground Nutmeg	30g	Rose Petals
2 tspn	Rosewater	1 tspn	Cornflour

Method

1. Boil all the ingredients, except the cornflour, for fifteen minutes.
2. Remove the cinnamon and the lemon.
3. Slacken the cornflour with a little cold water and whisk into the simmering soup.
4. Remove from heat and blend in a liquidizer and then pass through a fine sieve.
5. Check the seasoning and chill till required.
6. Garnish with some whipped cream or crème fraiche and a rose petal.

Note

In the main chapters of this book you will find salads and other dishes which utilize various flowers in the recipes.

BREAD & CHEESE

The bread throughout the land is made of such grain as the soil yeildeth, nevertheless the gentility commonly provide themselves sufficiently of wheat for their own tables, whilst their household and any poor neighbours in some shires are forced to content themselves with rye, or barley, yea and in time of dearth, many with bread made either of beans, peas or oats or of all together and some acorns among, of which scourge the poorest do soonest taste, sith they are least able to provide themselves of better. . . .

Holinshead's Chronicles 1577

"Eating the bitter bread of banishment"

Act iii Scene 1 *Richard 11*

A variety of breads were eaten in Elizabethan England. The rich ate bread made from fine white flour and baked at a low temperature giving a soft textured loaf called a Manchet. The lower classes ate coarser breads made from barley, rye or sometimes from dried peas, beans and oats, even mixed with acorns. These breads were baked at a higher temperature which produced much harder dark bread.

Types of Bread

Manchet was a small loaf made with fine white flour from wheat.

Cheat was also made from wheat but contained more bran which gave it a coarse texture and an off white to grey colour.

Ravelled Bread this was a coarse bread made from oats or beans or peas.

Brown or Black Bread was made from rye.

All types of bread sold by bakers had to conform in weight and shape to the law called **The Assize of Bread**, bakers had their own personal seal which had to be displayed on their loaves.

Speciality breads such as spiced or fruit loaves could only be baked at special times like Christmas, Good Friday or for funerals.

CHEESE

"I will make an end to my dinner
There's pippins and cheese to come"

Sir Hugh Evans
The Merry Wives of Windsor

Cheese has been made in Britain for over a thousand years. In the fourteenth century Monks refined the production methods and experimented with flavourings such as herbs and other seasonings.

From the sixteenth century English cheese was becoming known by the name of the region in which it was produced. Hard cheese was made with skimmed milk and soft cheese was made with full cream milk.

Dairy produce was considered an inferior food by the rich and was mostly consumed by the lower classes, who consumed cheese at breakfast with bread and butter and onions. Cheese was also the main ingredient in a type of ploughman's lunch, which was a favourite snack with the audiences at the Globe theatre during William Shakespeare's time.

Cheese Royale

Ingrdients

100g	Grated Cheese or Goat's Cheese	5g	Tewkesbury Mustard
3	Eggs	250ml	Cream
Seasoning to taste			

Method

1. Heat the cream and add the cheese, mix untill smooth.
2. Season the mix and add the mustard.
3. Pour the warm cream onto the eggs and mix in thoroughly, pour into a greased baking dish about 1" deep.
4. Bake in a Baine Marie in a moderate oven until set.
5. When set remove from Baine Marie and cool.
6. Turn out the Royale and cut into desired shape, can be served warm or cold with some toasted brioche, if required warm, just heat in a warm oven for 10 minutes.

CHEESE RECIPES

Warwickshire Muffins

Ingredients

4	Muffins - cut in half	200g	Grated Berkeswell Cheese
100g	Flour	100g	Butter
300ml	Full Cream Milk	30g	Tewkesbury Mustard
100g	Grated Apple	100g	Diced Smoked Bacon
4	Egg Yolks		Seasoning

Method

1. Melt butter and fry the bacon until cooked.
2. Add the flour and mix until the roux leaves the sides of the pan.
3. Gradually add the warmed milk, mix until smooth and add the cheese.
4. Add the apple and mustard and season. Cool slightly, add the egg yolks and remove from the heat and cool.
5. Pour into dish and refrigerate when cold.
6. Cut muffins in half and toast till crisp
7. Spread some of the cheese mixture onto each muffin and place under a grill until a brown crust forms.
8. Serve 2 pieces per portion.

The Globe Theatre Bite

Ingredients

100g	Grated Berkeswell Cheese	4	Eggs
½ pt	Double Cream	1 tsp	Mustard
100g	Sliced Onion	1 clove	Garlic - puréed
30g	Butter	20g	Chopped Chives
Pinch	Grated Nutmeg		Seasoning
200g	Short Pastry		

Method

1. Line a 8" flan ring with the pastry, dock and bake blind.
2. Sweat the onion and garlic in the butter and cool.
3. Mix the cream, eggs and cheese in a bowl, season and add the onion and garlic.
4. Pour mixture into a flan case and sprinkle with chives and nutmeg, bake in a moderate oven until set.
5. Cool and serve as required.

Manchet

Ingredients

550g	Strong Flour - half white, half wholemeal		
15g	Yeast	15g	Softened Butter
30g	Milk	250g	Luke Warm Water
	(mix milk and water together and warm)		
10g	Salt		

Method

1. Warm the flour. Cream the yeast in the warm water and milk.
2. Mix the butter with the liquid and add the salt, mix all with the flour.
3. Knead the dough until smooth. Allow to prove in a warm place - cover the bowl with cling film. Allow the dough to prove for 1 hour.
4. Divide the dough into two and mould into smooth rounds, place on a greased baking tray and allow to re-prove for 30 minutes.
5. Cut 2 slashes in the top of each loaf and bake in a preheated oven 220°C for about 30 minutes.
6. Cool on a wire cooling tray until required.

Milk Bread

Ingredients

15g	Yeast	15g	Caster Sugar
300ml	Warm Milk (blood heat)	500g	Strong Flour
10g	Salt	1	Egg Yolk

Method

1. Pre-heat oven to 200°C.
2. Cream yeast, sugar and milk together.
3. Sieve flour and salt into a bowl. Make a well in centre and add the rest of the wet ingredients, mix to a smooth dough.
4. Place dough back into bowl, cover with cling film and allow to prove for about 45 minutes until the dough has doubled in size.
5. Knead the dough again and shape into a loaf. Place in a greased and floured loaf tin, re-prove until the dough reaches the top of the tin.
6. Mix the egg yolk with a little milk and a pinch of salt, and brush liberally over the top of the dough before placing in a hot oven for about 45 minutes. When cooked and golden brown, turn on to a cooling wire and leave until cold.

Old English Rastons (Type of Brioche)

Ingredients

500g	Strong Flour		125g	Salt Free Butter
25g	Yeast		10g	Caster Sugar
3	Eggs		150g	Warm Milk
10g	Salt			

Method

1. Cream the yeast and sugar and mix with a little milk.
2. Sieve the flour and sugar into a bowl.
3. Make a well in the centre and add the yeast mixture and the milk and eggs, knead to a smooth dough.
4. Cut the butter into pieces and place on top of dough.
5. Preheat the oven to 200°C.
6. Cover with cling film and prove until doubled in size.
7. When proved, mix the butter into the dough and knead until smooth.
8. Mould into rolls or small round loaves and prove until double the size.
9. Place on a greased baking tray and egg wash the tops of the dough. Place in the oven and bake for 45 minutes.
10. Remove from the baking tray when cooked and cool.

Spiced Bread

Ingredients

125g	Wholemeal Flour		125g	Brown Flour
5g	Salt		30g	Baking Powder
10g	Ground Cinnamon		5g	Ground Ginger
10g	Ground Nutmeg		Pinch	Ground Cloves
Zest	of 1 Orange		2	Eggs
100ml	Milk		300ml	Honey
60g	Brown Sugar			

Method

1. Grease a large loaf tin and line with baking parchment.
2. Preheat oven to 200°C. Warm the honey and sugar until the sugar is dissolved, cool.
3. Sieve the flour and baking powder and salt into a bowl, add the spices and grated orange zest.
4. Make a well in centre and mix in the eggs and milk, add the cooled honey mixture. Stir until a smooth batter has formed.
5. Pour into loaf tin and bake in the oven for 90 minutes.
6. Check the bread and if it is colouring too much, cover with greased tin foil.
7. Check the bread with a skewer, if it comes out clean the bread is done.
8. Turn out onto a cooling wire and cool.

"Good wine is a good familiar creature, if it be well used"

Othello Moor of Venice.

"I would give all my fame for a pot of ale"

Henry V

Elizabethan Summer Sac

Ingredients

2	Wine Glasses of Sherry	2	Glasses of Fresh Orange Juice
60g	Caster Sugar - dissolved in 2 tablespoons of water		
4	Sliced Strawberries	4	Mint Leaves
	Crushed Ice		

Method

1. Mix the Sherry and Orange Juice with the cooled Sugar Syrup.
2. Pour into glasses, fill with crushed ice and decorate with Strawberries and Mint.
3. Serve with a straw.

Hamlet Crusta

Ingredients

1	Measure of Drambuie		½	Measure of Orange Juice
2	Tblsp. Lemon Juice			Icing Sugar
	Ice			

Method

1. Dip rim of glass in lemon juice and then icing sugar to form a crust on the rim.
2. Mix the Drambuie, orange and lemon juice and pour over ice into crusted glass.

Cider Cup

Ingredients

½ Ltr	Cider		1 glass	Sherry
½ glass	Brandy		½	Lemon - juice only
	Sugar to taste		Pinch	Nutmeg
	Borage Flowers			Crushed Ice

Method

1. Mix all wet ingredients, the sugar and spice together.
2. Add crushed ice and decorate with borage flowers.

Titania's Kiss

Ingredients

30g	Lemon Juice		60g	Vanilla Syrup
60g	Curacoa		60g	Yellow Chartreuse
60g	Brandy			

Method

1. Mix all together over shaved ice.

Blushing Juliet

Ingredients

½	Glass of Sherry	¼	Wine Glass Strawberry Syrup
¼	Juice of Lemon		Dash of Raspberry Coulis
	Shaved Ice	4	Raspberries

Method

1. Mix all together, pour into glass over shaved ice and decorate with raspberries.

Verona Lemonade

Ingredients

4	Lemons - peeled thinly & juice squeezed		
500g	Caster Sugar	70 cl	Sherry
1 Ltr	Water	½ Ltr	Milk

Method

1. Steep the lemon peel in the juice overnight
2. Mix the lemon juice, sugar, milk and water together, bring to the boil, add the Sherry and strain through muslin or a jelly bag until clear. Cool and serve very cold. Can be decorated with the lemons used for the peel, sliced thinly.

Puck's Pippin Punch

Ingredients

2	Apple - sliced thinly	1	Lemon - sliced thinly
25g	Caster Sugar	1	Bottle Good Red Wine

Method

1. Pour wine over the lemon and apples and add sugar, leave to stand for 3-4 hours.

BASIC RECIPES & CULINARY TECHNIQUES

STOCKS

White Chicken Stock

Ingredients

1.4kg	Chicken Carcase or Winglets	**200g**	Celery
200g	Carrot	**200g**	Onion
100g	Leek	**Bouquet** Garni	
2.5 Ltr	Water		

Method

1. Place the chicken in a deep pan and cover with the water, bring quickly to the boil and simmer.
2. Skim the scum from the surface using a slotted spoon.
3. Roughly chop the carrot, onion, celery and leek and add to the pot.
4. Add the bouquet garni and simmer for 1½ hours, skim frequently.
5. Pass through a fine strainer and cool as quickly as possible . Store in the fridge or freeze for future use.

Brown Chicken Stock

Ingredients

As for white chicken stock with **30g** of tomato paste.

Method

1. Brown the chicken carcase and the vegetables in the oven in a roasting tray.
2. Remove from the roasting tray, place in a deep pan and cover with water and tomato paste.
3. Cook as for white stock and strain.

Brown Beef or Veal Stock

Ingredients

2kg	Veal or Beef Bones - chopped small		
200g	Carrot	200g	Onion
100g	Celery	30g	Tomato Paste
1	Bouquet Garni	2 ½ Ltr	Water

Method

1. Roughly chop the carrot, onion and celery.
2. Roast the bones and vegetables in a hot oven until well browned.
3. Drain off any fat and place the bones and vegetables in a deep pan. Add the tomato paste and cover with the water.
4. Bring to the boil and simmer for three hours, skimming frequently.
5. Cool the stock and strain through a fine strainer.
6. Use as required.

Fish Stock

Ingredients

1kg	Fish bones (Sole or Turbot are best)		
100g	Onion - finely sliced	100g	Celery - chopped small
100g	Leek - white only, finely sliced	50g	Fennel - finely chopped
150ml	Dry White wine	10g	Parsley Stalks
½	Lemon - juice only	30g	Butter
2ltr	Water		

Method

1. Sweat the vegetables in the butter in a deep pan, wash the fish bones and add to the vegetables and cook for 5 minutes without colouring.
2. Add the wine, water and lemon juice and bring to the boil and simmer.
3. Add the parsley and skim frequently.
4. After simmering for 30 minutes, strain through a fine strainer and cool as quickly as possible. Use as required.

SAUCES

Vegetable Stock

Ingredients

500g	Carrot	200g	Celery
100g	Fennel	200g	Leek
200g	Onion	2ltr	Water
1	Bouquet Garni		

Method

1. Roughly chop all the vegetables.
2. Place all the vegetables in a deep pan and cover with the water, bring to the boil.
3. Add the bouquet garni and simmer for 45 minutes.
4. Pass through a fine strainer and cool as quickly as possible.
   Use as required.

White Butter Sauce

Ingredients

60g	Shallots ⁄ finely chopped	1 tblsp	White Wine Vinegar
4 tblsp	White Wine	2 tblsp	Cold Water
200g	Unsalted Butter ⁄ well chilled and diced small		
Squeeze Lemon Juice			

Method

1. Mix the shallots, wine vinegar and white wine in a shallow pan.
2. Boil the ingredients reducing the liquid to a syrup of about 1 tablespoon.
3. Add the cold water and gradually whisk in the butter making sure it is properly emulsified, do this over a low heat making sure the liquid does not boil.
4. Season with salt, ground white pepper and a little lemon juice.
5. The sauce can be served as it is, or strained.

White Wine Sauce (fish)

Ingredients

200ml	Fish Stock	60g	Finely Chopped Shallot
30g	Chopped Mushrooms	150ml	Double Cream
30g	Salt Free Butter		

Method

1. Sweat the shallots and the mushrooms in a little butter in a shallow pan, add the wine and reduce by 2/3 add the stock and bring to boil and reduce by ½.
2. Add the cream, reduce by 2/3 and whisk in the cold butter and season, do not reboil.
3. Strain through a fine strainer and use as soon as possible.

White or Red Wine Sauce (for Meat)

Ingredients

400ml	Beef or Veal Stock	200ml	White or Red Wine
60g	Finely Chopped Shallot	30g	Sliced Button Mushrooms
1tspn	Corn Flour	30g	Cold Diced Salt Free Butter.

Method

1. Place the shallots and mushrooms and wine in a shallow pan.
2. Bring to boil and reduce wine by 2/3, add the stock and reduce by ½ check seasoning,
3. Thicken the sauce with the corn flour and finish by whisking in the butter, do not re-boil.
4. Strain through a fine strainer or a muslin cloth.
   Use as required.

Hollandaise Sauce

Ingredients

250g	Salt Free Butter - melted, with lees removed (clarified)		
4	Egg yolks	**15ml**	White Wine Vinegar
30ml	Cold water	**5g**	Crushed White Peppercorns
Squeeze of Lemon Juice			

Method

1. To clarify the butter, heat very gently and pour off the clear butter leaving the milky residue behind.
2. In a shallow pan reduce the vinegar and peppercorns by 1/3.
3. Cool and add the water and the egg yolks. Whisk until fluffy then place over a low heat, whisking continuously. Make sure the whisk covers the whole base of the pan, the eggs should thicken and become creamy, do not over-heat or the eggs will curdle. This can also be done over a pan of hot water.
4. Remove from the heat and gradually incorporate the melted cooled butter, whisking continuously. Season and pass through a fine strainer, finish with lemon juice just before you serve.

Vinaigrette

Ingredients

100ml	Olive Oil	**30ml**	White Wine Vinegar
1tspn	Dijon Mustard		Squeeze Lemon
	Seasoning		

Method

1. Whisk all the ingredients together until they form an emulsion.
2. Season.

Mustard and Honey Dressing

Ingredients

100ml	Ground Nut Oil	**30ml**	White Wine Vinegar
2 tblesp	Honey	**1 tblesp**	Dijon Mustard

Method

1. Whisk all ingredients together to form an emulsion.

Tomato Dressing

Ingredients

50ml	Vinaigrette	**200g**	Chopped Tomatoes
5g	Caster Sugar	**4**	Basil Leaves

Method

1. Cut the tomatoes in ¼ and remove the seeds.
2. Finely chop the basil leaves.
3. Place all the ingredients in a liquidizer and blend together, season and use as required.

Mayonnaise

Ingredients

250ml	Olive Oil	**3**	Egg Yolks
1tspn	Dijon Mustard	**1tspn**	White Wine Vinegar.
Squeeze	Lemon Juice		Seasoning - salt and ground white pepper

Method

1. Whisk the eggs, mustard and vinegar in a bowl until they are light and have thickened.
2. Warm the oil slightly and whisk it into the eggs gradually. If the dressing becomes too thick add a little hot water and carry on whisking until all the oil is combined with the eggs.
3. Season and finish with lemon juice if required.

For best results remove eggs from the fridge to bring their temperature up before starting the dressing.

PASTRY

Short Crust Pastry

Ingredients

250g	Flour		65g	Unsalted Butter
60ml	Water		1	Egg Yolk
Pinch	Salt			

Method

1. Add the salt to the flour and sieve into a china bowl.
2. Rub the butter into the flour until it is a sandy texture, make a well in the centre and add the egg yolk combined with the water.
3. Knead to a smooth paste and form into a ball and wrap in cling film and rest as long as possible. Use as required.

Sweet Pastry / Germaine Paste

Ingredients

250g	Flour		2	Egg Yolks
75g	Icing Sugar		125g	Unsalted Butter
Pinch	Salt		2	Drops Vanilla Extract

Method

1. Cream the butter and sugar until white and creamy, add the vanilla extract.
2. Add the salt to the flour and fold into the eggs and butter.
3. Mix to a smooth paste and roll into a ball cover in cling film and rest for as long as possible, overnight would be best.
4. Roll out and use as required.

Shortbread Pastry

Ingredients

200g	Flour	50g	Cornflour
50g	Custard Powder	200g	Salt Free Butter
100g	Caster Sugar	4 drops	Vanilla Extract

Method

1. Combine all the ingredients together in a processor and mould into a ball. Rest before using.
2. Roll out to required shape.
3. Bake in a low oven until set, remove from oven and cool before moving the biscuits.

Stock Syrup (for poaching fruit)

Ingredients

500ml	Water	250g	Caster Sugar
1	Orange - peel only	1	Cinnamon Stick

Method

1. Place all the ingredients in a deep pan and bring to boil, stirring until the sugar is dissolved.
2. Simmer for 30 minutes and allow to cool, remove the peel and cinnamon before using.

Measure For Measure
Conversion Charts

Imperial	Metric	American

Solid Measure

Imperial	Metric	American
½ oz	12.5g	1 tablespoon
1 oz	25g	2 tablespoons
4 oz	100g	½ cup
8 oz	200g	1 cup
16 oz	400g	2 cups

Liquid Measure

Imperial	Metric
1 fl oz	30ml
2 fl oz	60ml
5 fl oz	150ml
10 fl oz	300ml
20 fl oz	600ml
35 fl oz	1 litre

Approximate Size Chart

½ cm	¼ inch
1 cm	½ inch
2 cm	1 inch
4 cm	2 inch
5 cm	2 ½ inches
8 cm	4 inches
10 cm	5 inches
24 cm	12 inches

Temperature Charts

Gas Mark	Celsius	Fahrenheit	Remark
¼	110	225	Cool
½	130	250	
1	140	275	
2	150	300	
3	160	325	
4	180	350	Moderate
5	190	375	
6	200	400	
7	220	425	Hot
8	230	450	
9	250	475	Very Hot

Ballotine	A leg of chicken or a whole bird with all bones removed, stuffed and tied for cooking.
Bain Marie	Using a tray as a water bath in the oven to keep the temperature steady and prevent some products curdling. Also a water bath on top of stove for keeping sauces warm, and helping them cook out.
Bake Blind	Baking a pastry case without filling, using dried beans to keep the base flat.
Bard	To cover the breast of poultry or game birds with bacon to keep them moist.
Baste	To spoon the hot cooking fat over the article being roasted.
Blanch	To bring to the boil and then refresh in cold water, or to cook something like chips without colouring, or to remove the skin from a tomato by plunging it into boiling water for 10 seconds then refreshing it in cold water.
Batons	Strips of vegetable or meat 2 cm x .25 cm size.
Bouquet Garni	A selection of herbs, parsley, thyme and bay leaf tied in muslin cloth or leek leaf to give flavour to stocks, soups, stews and sauces.
Chiffonade	Fine strips of spinach, lettuce or sorrel.
Clarified Butter	Butter melted and strained removing the milky solids.
Concassée	Tomatoes with the skin and pips removed, diced.
Confit	Vegetables, fruit or meat cooked till it is thick and syrupy.
Coulis	A purée made from fruit or vegetables for a sauce.
Dariole	A metal mould used to set mousse or other ingredients into a fez shape.
De glaze	To swill the cooking pan out with wine or stock to remove the sediment and help flavour a sauce.
Duxelles	Finely chopped shallot and mushrooms, cooked and used as a stuffing.

Emulsion	A mixture of oil and wine, vinegar or stock, whisked until they amalgamate.
Flambé	To ignite alcohol fumes with a naked flame.
Julienne	Thin strips of vegetables or meat ⁃ like a match stick.
Larding	To insert strips of fat or bacon into meat to add flavour.
Marinade	A liquid used to soak ingredients in so as to add flavour or tenderize.
Mirepoix	Roughly chopped vegetables used as a base in braising, stews and stocks.
Mulled	Flavoured and spiced wine or cider.
Prunelle	A plum flavoured liqueur
Ramekin	Small porcelain dishes used for baking and setting a variety of dishes.
Reduce	To concentrate the flavour of stocks and sauces by boiling the liquid rapidly.
Refresh	To cool something rapidly in cold water.
Roux	Equal quantities of butter and flour, cooked together and used to thicken soups, sauces and stews.
Sabayon	A mixture of egg yolks whisked over heat until light and fluffy, used for Hollandaise type sauces and sweets.
Sauté	To cook quickly in a frying or sauté pan colouring the article being cooked
Seared	To quickly cook on both sides.
Seal	To quickly colour meat in a frying pan to keep in the juices.
Slake	To dilute a starch such as cornflour, arrowroot, or potato starch with water before thickening a sauce or soup or stew.
Sweat	To cook in a pan without colour.
Tamp	To compress something in a mould to form a specific shape.
Velouté	A velvet textured soup using a blond roux and stock.